The Way of the Urban Monk

"For far too long, many of us Christians have divided ourselves into 'spiritual' types or 'social justice' types, as if the two were somehow incompatible. Joe Colletti definitively unites the two. This book shows the reader not only how to find the best place for one's own ministry but also how to build one's unique integrated rule of life. A fine route to harmonious complexity."

—**Norvene Vest**, author of *Claiming Your Voice: Speaking Truth to Power*

"Inspiring. This book merges the seemingly disparate worlds of urban living and monk-like discipline and offers a fresh perspective on addressing societal challenges, and it emphasizes the importance of inner spiritual depth alongside practical action. A valuable resource for anyone seeking to navigate the complexities of urban life while making a meaningful impact on society."

—**Young Lee Hertig**, executive director, Innovative Space for Asian American Christianity

"The book that many of us have been waiting for: a nuanced, experience-based guidebook that integrates social justice activity and spiritual disciplines practice. Well written, highly accessible, theologically astute, and alive with personal illustrations. I can see this book being used not only in theological seminaries and universities but in local churches with an urban vision. It has the potential to be life changing."

—**Richard Peace**, senior professor of evangelism and spiritual formation, Fuller Theological Seminary

"This book marks a significant contribution to the subjects of spirituality, theology, social change, and Christian spiritual praxis. It is not simply one person's theory; it is the theoretical brought to life. It will enrich the lives of anyone who takes the time to read it."

—**Cecil M. Robeck Jr.**, director, Center for Christian Spirituality, Fuller Theological Seminary

"*The Way of the Urban Monk* provides a welcome distillation of the integral relationship between spirituality and social activism. Reflecting on his own journey and tapping into spiritual principles and both ancient and contemporary practices, Joe Colletti provides a practical guide toward forming a personal integrated rule of life, a practice for anyone desiring a spirituality that informs and sustains a commitment to making our world a better one, especially for those on the margins."

—**MICHAEL A. MATA**, pastor for community engagement,
Los Angeles First Church of the Nazarene

The Way of the Urban Monk

A Spirituality for Solving Social Injustice

Joe Colletti

Foreword by Wil Hernandez

CASCADE *Books* • Eugene, Oregon

THE WAY OF THE URBAN MONK
A Spirituality for Solving Social Injustice

Copyright © 2024 Joe Colletti. All rights reserved. Except for brief quotations in critical publications or reviews, no part of this book may be reproduced in any manner without prior written permission from the publisher. Write: Permissions, Wipf and Stock Publishers, 199 W. 8th Ave., Suite 3, Eugene, OR 97401.

Cascade Books
An Imprint of Wipf and Stock Publishers
199 W. 8th Ave., Suite 3
Eugene, OR 97401

www.wipfandstock.com

PAPERBACK ISBN: 979-8-3852-0248-5
HARDCOVER ISBN: 979-8-3852-0249-2
EBOOK ISBN: 979-8-3852-0250-8

Cataloguing-in-Publication data:

Names: Colletti, Joe [author]. | Hernandez, Wil [foreword writer]

Title: The way of the urban monk : a spirituality for solving social injustice / Joe Colletti.

Description: Eugene, OR: Cascade Books, 2024 | Includes bibliographical references.

Identifiers: ISBN 979-8-3852-0248-5 (paperback) | ISBN 979-8-3852-0249-2 (hardcover) | ISBN 979-8-3852-0250-8 (ebook)

Subjects: LCSH: Church and social problems. | Monasticism and religious life. | Spiritual formation. | Spiritual life—Christianity. | Christianity and justice. | Social justice.

Classification: BX2435 C65 2024 (paperback) | BX2435 (ebook)

VERSION NUMBER 10/07/24

To the many social reformers whose lives and legacies continue to shape my understanding and experiences of the interaction between spirituality and social justice to collectively overcome injustices.

Contents

Foreword by Wil Hernandez | ix
Introduction | 1

1. An Integrated Rule of Life: Your Map to Effective Spiritually Informed Social Justice | 13
2. Choosing Your Social Struggle | 22
3. Spiritual Principles: Discerning the Values That Will Light Your Way | 34
4. Disciplined Spiritual Practices, Part 1: Divine Office of Prayer, Daily Examen, and Lectio Divina | 50
5. Disciplined Spiritual Practices, Part 2: Silence, Centering Prayer, and Theological Reflection | 67
6. Convictional Spiritual Practices | 76
7. Impassioned Spiritual Practices | 87
8. Merging the Sacred and the Secular for Social Action | 99
9. Leaving a Lasting Spiritual Legacy | 120

Appendix: A Lectio Divina Practice for Social Justice | 127
Bibliography | 133

Foreword

Henri Nouwen, whom I consider to be my patron saint, penned a riveting foreword to Gustavo Gutiérrez's highly influential, seminal work on liberation theology some three decades ago. In *We Drink Our Own Wells: The Spiritual Journey of a People*, after echoing the author's own articulation of what spirituality is about as "like a living water that springs up in the very depths of the experience of faith,"[1] Nouwen follows it with his interpretation of what Gutiérrez means: "To drink from your own well is to live your own life in the Spirit of Jesus as you have encountered him in your concrete historical reality." These opening remarks of Nouwen set the context for the following admission he then issues so transparently a couple of pages later:

> But as I reflect on the impact of this spirituality on my own way of living and thinking, I realize that a reductionism has taken place on my side.... I became aware of how individualistic and elitist my own spirituality had been. It was hard to confess, but true, that in many respects my thinking about the spiritual life had been deeply influenced by the North American milieu with its emphasis upon the "interior life" and the methods and techniques for developing that life. Only when I confronted what Gustavo calls the "irruption of the poor into history" did I become aware of how "spiritualized" my spirituality had become. It had been, in fact, a spirituality for introspective persons who have the luxury of the time and space needed to develop inner harmony and quietude.[2]

I remember something got pricked inside of me the first time I read Nouwen's public confession. Without a doubt, I could relate—and I would

1. Nouwen, foreword to *We Drink from Our Own Wells*.
2. Nouwen, *We Drink from Our Own Wells*.

Foreword

hazard to guess, many others resonate with it. Indeed, it is so easy to pursue a highly privatized and interiorized brand of spirituality devoid of any kind of public engagement with the world we live in. To my own shame, I am not exempt from this all-prevailing tendency of so many of us involved in promoting Christian spirituality to succumb to this lopsided mindset.

A little more than a decade ago, I founded CenterQuest (CQ), an ecumenical hub for the study and practice of Christian spirituality, with its School of Spiritual Direction (SSD) hybrid program as its main thrust. Luckily, Joe Colletti, a longtime friend prior to its launching, was there to lend his all-out support for our new endeavor. As a close ally, I felt it right for me to return the favor by also supporting his much earlier initiative of spearheading the Society of the Urban Monks. Through my own involvement with his outfit over the years, I have come to appreciate the commitment to lived-out spirituality that we share in common. Increasingly, too, I have become more keenly aware of how our two organizations could help strengthen each other in mutual and complementary ways. In fact, on numerous occasions over the years, we've had lots of brainstorming chats on a variety of possible ways by which we can more concretely collaborate together for our respective organization's mutual benefit.

More recently, on our end, our CenterQuest program leadership, after running five cohort cycles of our School of Spiritual Direction, deemed that it's about time to include in our curriculum a module on spiritual direction and social justice. Again, after much deliberation and consultation with Joe, we finally came up with the initial idea of field-testing an online course under CQ's Lifelong Learning Community (LLC) on the topic of "Public Engagement: Integrating Spiritual Principles and Practices for Solving Social Struggles" and offering this to all our SSD cohort graduates. Joe and I started working together to design the course, which is mainly based on a number of writings he has developed over the years, to be facilitated by him. Due to the pandemic and other unforeseeable circumstances, the implementation of our pilot project got delayed. In the interim, Joe focused his attention into turning his seminal writings into a book, which is what you are now holding in your hand.

It is therefore with much excitement that I recommend very highly this book, which is a product of Joe's lifelong efforts and commitment to rally all of us who are engaged in the work of spiritual formation and spirituality toward a form of public engagement aimed at balancing the inward and the outward dimensions of our spiritual life. Like Henri Nouwen under

Foreword

Gutierrez's influence, we seek to advocate not a bifurcation but a more practical integration between contemplation and action, between the mystical and the prophetic, between solitude and community, between prayer and service and, really, to highlight the indivisible thrust of the love commandment itself: between love of God and love of our neighbor.

Joe is more than qualified to address this issue of integrating spirituality and social concern, which many of us are most prone to dichotomize. As a social reformer who has modeled his life in the tradition of past and contemporary social reformers, Joe has dedicated his life to solving social problems that often stem from poverty, prejudice, and parochialism. He has worked fervently with many cities and counties throughout California to prevent and end homelessness and has helped develop and implement many local jurisdictional plans and programs founded on evidence-based, best, emerging, and promising practices that have resulted in thousands of homeless people exiting their state of homelessness. He has also worked passionately with numerous nonprofit organizations and congregations to design and implement programs and projects based on practices to help solve social injustices in the communities in which they serve. Such practices include creating coalitions made up of representatives of local government and community organizations which commit to long-term cooperation to achieve solutions to the problems they want to resolve.

Aside from being the cofounder and chief executive officer of the Hub for Urban Initiatives, together with his wife, Sofia Herrera, a clinical psychologist by training, they cofounded the Center for Urban Initiatives at Fuller Theological Seminary, where he also has served as an adjunct associate professor of urban studies. His teaching focused primarily on the integration of Christian monastic practices and solving social struggles. Much of his community and economic development efforts address, from the human rights and social justice angle, the issues of affordable housing, economic development, fair housing, health and mental health care, homelessness, human trafficking, and substance abuse.

In 2006, Joe established the Society of Urban Monks, which is an ecumenical and multidenominational community of men and women who are involved in encountering, engaging, and ending social issues and injustices by infusing their Christian faith and spiritual practices into their employment, education, social, and volunteer efforts and activities. Anyone can become an urban monk by living out spiritual principles and practices as

Foreword

a means to nurture a deep, collective, and public relationship with God to help encounter, engage, and end social injustices.

In the past, I've had several opportunities to participate in the monastic mass that the Society used to conduct regularly. On a few occasions, my wife and I, along with other invited friends, have enjoyed having sacred meals that he and Sofia have hosted in their home, which incorporated the practice of evening and night prayers.

In conjunction with the notion of the urban monk, Joe has labored passionately to put together in book form his vision for the urban monk emerging from his personal conviction that, as people of faith, it is imperative that we promote civic engagement. According to him, the way of an urban monk involves creating and cultivating an integrated rule of life that includes the following three elements: nurturing an intimate, personal, and private relationship with God; extending charity to others; and moving beyond individual acts of charity by engaging in community efforts to achieve justice and right social wrongs.

As a practicing spiritual director involved in companioning others in their journey of faith in a holistic manner, I endorse his work enthusiastically. I believe that anyone involved in the work of formation can profit much from the core message of the book along with its highly practical applications. In fact, what I particularly like about it is that each chapter is capped by carefully written reflection questions to help the reader personalize and internalize each aspect of what is involved in crafting one's rule of life.

I personally share Joe's sincere hope that as a result of engaging the contents of this material, we, the readers, can be inspired and all the more motivated to imbibe in our hearts the way of the urban monk—by identifying the spiritual principles that will inform and fortify our efforts and selecting the spiritual practices that will help sustain our commitment to social justice work as an integral part of our lived spirituality.

—**Wil Hernandez**, PhD, Obl. OSB
executive director, CenterQuest
author, *Mere Spirituality: The Spiritual Life According to Henri Nouwen*

Introduction

THIS BOOK IS ABOUT becoming an urban monk—an ordinary person who wants to live an extraordinary life by crafting a rule of life that integrates personally chosen, biblically rooted spiritual principles and practices into efforts to help achieve solutions for social injustices.

Urban monks do more than charitable work in their neighborhoods, communities, cities, and counties where others are trying to solve social struggles. They integrate their spirituality into all they do to help enact lasting reforms and bring an end to social injustices. Spirituality is generally practiced privately or collectively among family, friends, and alongside others in settings like home study groups, retreats, or congregations. However, many socially conscious Christians are not practicing their spirituality in a public way, which is necessary to help shape solutions for social struggles. More of us need to do so if we are to bring an end to seemingly intractable social problems. As urban monks, having an integrated rule of life can help us bring our spirituality to the center of every aspect of our lives and sustain us in the challenging work of ending social injustice.

Spirituality Defined

Spirituality is often described as a personal yearning to connect with something greater than ourselves, a deep longing to find meaning and purpose in our lives, which is arguably a universal human experience that stirs all of us. We turn inward in our search to understand and connect with the human spirit or soul, and to cultivate a deep, private relationship with God.

We often seek to develop our spiritual lives from a need to cope with change or uncertainty and from a craving for peace and comfort in life.

The desire to be connected to something bigger than ourselves may be an immediate need because of a tragic event or other experiences that have left us wounded and hurting. We may be experiencing abandonment by others, including those closest to us or those charged with our well-being.

In the context of this book, I expand spirituality beyond the inward personal journey. The need to be connected to something bigger than ourselves can include others if we allow it to. Thus, we not only turn to our spirituality to cope with change or uncertainty for ourselves but for others as well, whether they be family members, friends, coworkers, acquaintances, or strangers. In this broader view of spirituality, we acknowledge that the craving for peace and comfort is experienced by all those around us and we aim to help others share in it. This expansive spirituality helps us deepen our awareness of the hurts and pains that have left the people in our communities affronted and wounded. With it we foster a greater consciousness of their abandonment by others, including ourselves. As the Benedictine monk Brother David Steindl-Rast explains,

> Sometimes people get the mistaken notion that spirituality is a separate department of life, the penthouse of our existence. But rightly understood, it is a vital awareness that pervades all realms of our being.... Wherever we come alive, that is the area in which we are spiritual.... To be vital, awake, aware, in all areas of our lives is the task that is never accomplished but it remains the goal.

The urban monk comes alive working with others to find lasting solutions to all manner of social injustice: homelessness, food insecurity, systemic racism, social inequality, inequitable access to health care and education, and more. Their spirituality is a personal source of sustenance and renewal but also a sacred fuel to inspire and engage all levels of communal involvement to heal our most pervasive social struggles.

The Urban Monk's Broad View and Commitment to Lasting Change

The urban monk's spirituality infuses everything they do, including public engagement, and is a driving force for their efforts in their communities. They are committed to working with others and inspiring them to solve some of our society's most challenging problems, and they rely on their Christian faith and spiritual principles and practices to support them in what is often a lifetime commitment.

Introduction

Make no mistake—the urban monk's public expression of their spirituality is different from proselytizing. They are not trying to convert people to the Christian faith or beliefs. Rather, urban monks employ spiritual principles and practices to aid them in their efforts in the secular community—for example, for strength, focus, and direction as they serve on coalitions, committees, and councils committed to solving social struggles.

More than a source of personal nourishment, spiritual principles and practices can also guide and sustain the urban monk's work with others in influencing, implementing, and innovating solutions for highly complex societal problems. Such values and ethical practices include faith, hope, and love, which are foundational in the Christian Scriptures. When one doubts that a seemingly intractable social struggle can be solved, faith instills confidence that a solution can be found. Hope normalizes doubt by energizing confidence and conviction. Love is essential, especially when serving some of the most vulnerable members of our communities as well as when serving with others in highly charged environments of competing opinions, personal and professional agendas, and often limited resources.

The work involved in helping to end social injustice often brings together disparate sectors of our communities: those who are hurt and those who inflicted the hurt, those who feel unheard and those who are being accused of turning a deaf ear. The urban monk practices the Christian values of forgiveness and acceptance to help them navigate diverse personalities, perspectives, and experiences. And none of their efforts can be carried out or sustained without humility—not thinking less of oneself but thinking of oneself less.

The urban monk's spirituality motivates them to change lives and ultimately the conditions within the communities around them. They listen, interact, implement, and inspire within educational institutions, faith-based groups, local government task forces, and nonprofit organizations, as well as secular civic coalitions, committees, and commissions. By interweaving their community efforts with their spiritual principles and practices, urban monks serve as working models for how spirituality in action can heal the world.

To guide and sustain them in this work, urban monks rely on an integrated rule of life. In the traditional Christian sense, a rule of life is a personal living covenant with God. It documents the solemn promises and spiritual renewal between God and the individual. The spiritual principles and practices found in the Christian Scriptures and rooted in the passion of Jesus Christ form the foundation of an integrated rule of life.

The purpose of this book is to walk you through developing your own integrated rule of life. Each chapter examines one aspect of an integrated rule of life and shows how you can draw from your experience, faith, aspirations, and passion to craft a personal spiritual tool to help you in your efforts to solve seemingly intractable social struggles and deepen your relationship with God.

Why I Wrote This Book

My motivation to write this book stems from my belief that spiritual principles and ancient and contemporary spiritual practices should be intentionally integrated into efforts to solve social struggles. I came to this belief through personal and professional experience.

Throughout this book, I will share my experiences of discovering—or rediscovering—biblically rooted spiritual principles and practices as I worked with others to address community challenges, including homelessness, housing discrimination, and neighborhood disinvestment. As our collective journey unfolded, and at the suggestion of a spiritual director, I began to develop a "rule of life" that included practices such as lectio divina, the Divine Office of Prayer, and the daily examen.

My spiritual life evolved along with my professional life and my involvement in what at first appeared to be secular activities—participating in community coalitions; creating new coalitions; and completing many homelessness affordable housing and neighborhood disinvestment assessments and strategies for communities, cities, and counties. I also worked on assessments and strategies that focused on ending housing and land-use discrimination as well as on economic reinvestment in small businesses. In the midst of these efforts, I worked with others to draft recommendations based on community data generated from locally crafted surveys, focus groups, and federal, state, county, and city sources, which we included in our assessments and strategies to address these social wrongs.

I then worked with others to develop residential and nonresidential programs for people experiencing homelessness. We also developed affordable housing projects and established sidewalk vending districts and kitchen incubators for small food-based businesses. I wrote many federal,

Introduction

state, and local grant applications each year that secured funds to help carry out the recommendations.

The more I engaged in these activities, the more I felt the need to integrate spiritual principles and practices with my efforts to help solve social struggles. For years I had crafted a rule of life that helped me cultivate an intimate, personal, and private relationship with God and loving relationships with family, friends, and coworkers. As I continued to engage with the issues I cared so deeply about, I discovered that my work had taken on a sacred dimension.

I began to see the urban world as my monastery. The idea for this book emerged from my experiences and zeal to continuously revise my rule of life to meet contemporary urban challenges by integrating principles and practices into my unceasing efforts to work with community partners to encounter, engage, and end social problems and injustices. Thus, my rule of life evolved into an *integrated* rule of life.

I was also motivated to familiarize myself with the efforts and accomplishments of social reformers of the past, many of whom remain unknown to (or are forgotten by) those who seek to advance social justice today. This oversight has left us poorer in our current efforts. Among the many reformers I read and studied was Jacob A. Riis, who exposed the horrible living and working conditions of poor immigrants in New York City through his journalism and photography in the late nineteenth century. Because of Riis's leadership, health and sanitation laws were passed and enforced as philanthropic organizations and special commissions investigated the abuses revealed by his photographs. The city adopted housing codes that required fire escapes, windows, toilets, and running water. Existing housing was upgraded or razed, depending on current conditions. By the time he died in 1914, Riis was known as the "Emancipator of the Slums."

I was also inspired by the social reformer Nellie Bly, a pioneer of investigative journalism. She posed as a mental health patient in a women's boarding house and a mental asylum in New York City and wrote about her horrendous experiences of cruel beatings, ice-cold baths, and forced meals filled with spoiled and vermin-infested foods. Her stories created an uproar in New York and were syndicated throughout the country, spurring a national outcry that catalyzed mental healthcare reforms throughout the United States.

I was also deeply inspired by the work of Martin Luther King Jr., whose preaching and leadership of nonviolent protests during the civil rights movement led to decisive legislative gains in the Civil Rights Act of 1964, the Voting Rights Act of 1965, and the Fair Housing Act of 1968. In turn, these gains helped shape later legislation, including the Equal Employment Opportunity Act of 1972 and the Americans with Disabilities Act of 1990.

The Society of Urban Monks

The idea of urban monasticism guided by the integrated rule of life grew as I created the Society of Urban Monks, an active worldwide community of people who are involved in solving social struggles in their communities, cities, regions, and countries. Each urban monk is committed to living out their own rule of life as they integrate personally chosen spiritual principles and practices into their efforts to help solve seemingly intractable social struggles over time. We take our inspiration from past social reformers by sharing and recommending their written works.

The Society started as a gathering of friends and coworkers around my dining room table. My wife and I would invite a dozen or so people to each seder-like meal. Full of symbolism and storytelling, the dinner would begin with a reading of a psalm that focused on justice. We would then pass around a piece of parsley, and each person would dip it in their glass of water and shake it over their salad to convey the drops of water as the tears that are shed by those who are experiencing injustices. Then, with the salad, we would pass around the saltshaker as each one of us would shake a little salt on our salad as we remembered that Christ taught us to be the salt of the earth (Matt 5:1–13).

I soon began inviting those same dinner guests, along with students from the urban studies classes I taught at Fuller Theological Seminary, to a "monastic mass" I led once a month at a friend's local church.

I called our service a monastic mass because the liturgy, which I wrote, included several monastic practices: chanting, lectio divina, and periods of silence and reflection. The sacred readings always included Scripture passages that called for justice. We also dedicated time to allow each participant to briefly note a local or worldwide injustice of concern.

I called us "urban monks," which everyone liked. Thus, our once-a-month monastic masses became the public gathering of the Society of Urban Monks. Soon I created a website, a newsletter, and a listserv that included people interested in joining the Society. As the listserv grew, so

Introduction

did the number of people who joined the Society. Soon there were urban monks who lived in countries across the world.

By reading this book and developing your own integrated rule of life, you are poised to join the Society of Urban Monks and codify the spiritual principles and practices that shape and nourish your work and spirit. Your integrated rule of life will become for you—as it did for me—a living, growing, strengthening organism to continuously mature your relationship with God. As a source of continual spiritual renewal, it will heighten your ability to be an agent of change and healing in the communities in which you live, work, worship, recreate, socialize, and serve. It will strengthen your abilities to love your neighbor as yourself and to express an intense love for an entire community, city, county, or country as you increase your stamina to work for solutions to social struggles.

Mapping the Path Forward

In each chapter of this book, I examine one aspect of an integrated rule of life and how it to can support you in your efforts to find solutions to social injustice. I draw from the Christian Scriptures, the writings of spiritual luminaries of many denominations of the Christian faith, and the work of the social reformers who serve as our society's most powerful examples of being the force for positive change. I also share from my decades of experience as a social reformer working with numerous cities and counties to solve social struggles, as well as from my roles as chief executive officer of the Hub for Urban Initiatives, adjunct associate professor of urban studies at Fuller Theological Seminary, and cofounder and codirector of Fuller's Center for Urban Initiatives.

Chapter 1 provides spiritual and historical context for an integrated rule of life. It calls out examples of the mystics and social reformers who have demonstrated for us what it looks like to live out an intimate relationship with God, integrate spiritual principles and practices with social action, and further the teachings of Christ and the tradition of Christian reform by becoming agents of change and healing. The chapter gets us started crafting our own spiritual guidelines by closely examining the three foundational elements of an integrated rule of life: nurturing an intimate, personal, and private relationship with God; extending charity to others; and moving beyond individual acts of charity by committing to working with others in long-term community efforts to achieve justice and right social wrongs.

Urban monks are committed to solving, with others, social injustices in the communities and cities in which they live, work, worship, recreate, socialize, and serve. Therefore one of the first steps in becoming an urban monk and designing your integrated rule of life is to choose the social struggles that you want to help solve with others. No city or town in the United States is untouched by social injustice of some kind: child abuse, racism and inequality, healthcare disparity, homelessness, human trafficking, hunger, climate change, crime, education disparities, substance abuse, and unemployment. No one person can tackle them all, so chapter 2 helps you discern your primary focus. It guides you to explore the social struggles that personally impact you or those close to you: family members, friends, classmates, and coworkers. You will mine your education, whether formal or informal, for areas of social justice work that especially spoke to your mind and heart. You will reflect on the people—living or from the past—you look up to as examples of individuals bettering our world. Finally, you will identify where in your everyday life you have seen or felt compassion, or felt most energized, purposeful, and satisfied with your efforts.

With the pervasiveness of social injustice, choosing your social struggle is not so easy to do. We want to end all suffering, not just the suffering of the homeless or the hungry or those who are discriminated against. The examples in chapter 2, including my experience as a social worker for the City of Pasadena's Bad Weather Shelter, illustrate the benefits of honing your focus. It takes time to understand the nuances of these complex issues, to learn the tools available for enacting change, and to become familiar with the networks of people and resources to tap in order to make progress in what is sure to be a long-term commitment.

Spiritual principles, a foundational building block for any integrated rule of life, deepen our understanding of social wrongs. As we cultivate them over time, these spiritual principles spur and sustain our courage and commitment to right the wrongs. Chapter 3 helps you identify the spiritual principles that will factor into your rule of life. It looks at some core Christian spiritual principles—faith, hope, love, forgiveness, acceptance, reconciliation, humility, integrity, honor, service, grace, and discernment—and shows how they may guide and fortify you specifically in your efforts to solve social injustice.

Introduction

Spiritual practices—disciplined, convictional, and impassioned—help us sustain our commitment to solving social injustices and deepen our relationship to the work, to those we work with and for, and to God. Chapters 4 and 5 examine the disciplined spiritual practices: the Divine Office of Prayer, the daily examen, lectio divina, silence, centering prayer, and theological reflection. These chapters show how these practices, when incorporated into a rule of life and practiced regularly, can help quiet your mind and spirit, offer you respite and renewal, and create sacred space in which to transform your daily activities and interactions into healing dialogue with God.

Chapter 6 explores convictional spiritual practices, exercises that express firmly held attitudes or beliefs that compel us to action and are energized by glimpses of solutions for seemingly intractable social ills and issues. Incarnational solidarity, the wounded healer, and the integration of material and spiritual poverty reflect an attitude rooted in the idea that our lives and all that we have should be shared with others—whether we know them or not. Integrating our everyday interactions with the intention of reconciliation has the potential for long-overdue healing. And as a convictional concept, the monastic cell provides a space not to escape from the world but rather to access our soul—the place we can continually discover, affirm, empower, and transform our loving service to God and others. As part of an integrated rule of life, convictional spiritual practices can help prepare us and ultimately move us into action, which is crucial for civic engagement.

Chapter 7 examines impassioned spiritual practices, which are disciplined spiritual practices that are emotionally resonant and highly personalized when they are practiced in reflection of what you're deeply passionate about. For urban monks, this is often focused around the social injustice to which they've dedicated their lives and work to solving: the cause itself, the people they serve, and the people they work with. As such, as part of an integrated rule of life, these impassioned practices can continuously nourish and renew the urban monk's spirit and commitment to their chosen social struggle. To illustrate impassioned spiritual practices within the life of an urban monk, I share my practices of praying with the Psalms, combining the Divine Office of Prayer with blues music, reading the passionate love prayers of the church mystics, transforming a restless night of sleep into a beneficial time to commune with God, embracing the dark night of the soul, and practicing groaning to express a sense of helplessness when I do not know what to pray for and I need the Spirit to intercede. As I explain in chapter 7, my impassioned spiritual practices stem from the various ways prayer and Scripture reading are practiced today, which evolved out of the way others began praying decades or even centuries ago. But any spiritual practice can become impassioned when infused with the fire to enact lasting change and transformative healing for ourselves and others.

We live our rule of life when we integrate our spiritual principles and practices with our secular life, specifically our efforts to help find solutions to social injustices and bring healing to the world, starting with our own community. In chapter 8, I share some ways that I live out my rule of life as a fulcrum for social action, specifically related to the social struggle of homelessness. In it you will see how I engage some of my chosen spiritual principles and practices in the secular world with the goal of enacting lasting social reform. In doing so, I hope to provide you with inspiration to further develop and evolve your rule of life, to stay committed to your chosen struggle, and to deepen your spiritual life and relationship with God.

Finally, in chapter 9, you'll learn how your integrated rule of life can become a distinctive spiritual legacy, one that can help ordinary people live extraordinary lives by guiding them to nurture a deep personal and collective relationship with God in order to encounter and engage social injustices and work to end them. You will be encouraged to live your rule of life, treating it as a living, growing, strengthening organism, so that it serves as a beacon for future generations called to the tireless work of lasting social reform. You will be inspired to coach others to build their own integrated rule of life by sharing the spiritual principles and practices you chose to integrate into your efforts as an urban monk and the formative moments and experiences that brought about lifelong changes in yourself and others. In order to do this, you will be encouraged to document your journey in a journal of some kind, describing the social struggles you committed to, the spiritual principles and practices that sustained you in this work, obstacles on your path and what helped you overcome them, and victories you've achieved in your efforts to help others.

Build and Share

In the beginning, crafting an integrated rule of life may feel like an enormous task. To help you get started, each chapter concludes with a list of reflection questions to help you personalize and internalize each aspect of your rule of life. These questions are intended to help you choose the

Introduction

primary focus of your social justice, identify the spiritual principles that will inform and fortify your efforts, and select the spiritual practices that will help sustain your commitment to social justice work and deepen your relationships with those you work with and for, as well as with God.

To help you contemplate these questions, I encourage you to keep a journal in which you can record your response and reactions. All you need is a blank notebook and something to write with. (You can also keep a digital journal on your personal computer, tablet, or phone.) Along with your responses to the book's questions, your journal can be a place to document the spiritual practices that motivated and prepared you for community action, soothed a yearning to spend time with God, or helped you handle challenging relationship dynamics encountered within a committee in which you serve. You might use your journal as a daily dialogue with God, capturing the prayers and Scripture excerpts that spoke most powerfully to you on a given day or through which you were able to feel God's guiding presence. You may find it helpful as a place to describe the role your relationship with God plays in navigating the complex emotions and opinions—yours and others'—that you encounter in your work to implement change.

Many spiritual luminaries and social reformers kept journals. St. Ignatius of Loyola kept a journal that became the *Spiritual Exercises*. The journal of St. Therese of Lisieux was published as *The Story of a Soul* and became a modern spiritual classic. Often these well-known journalers tout the power of writing as a tool for spiritual growth. For example, the book *Inner Voice of Love* is the diary Henri Nouwen kept from 1987 to 1988. During this time Nouwen was clinically depressed, but he found his journal to be a source of strength. "To my surprise," he wrote, "I never lost the ability to write. In fact, writing became part of my struggle for survival. It gave me the little distance from myself that I needed to keep from drowning in my despair."

Journaling quiets the mind, provides a safe space in which to process emotions, and documents your spiritual journey—a history that you can return to for insight and wisdom. In *The Sign of Jonas*, Thomas Merton's journal covering five years of his life (1946 to 1952) as a monk at the Abbey of Our Lady of Gethsemani, explains some of journaling's benefits:

> Keeping a journal has taught me that there is not so much new in your life as you sometimes think. When you re-read your journal you find out that your latest discovery is something you already found out five years ago. Still, it is true that one penetrates deeper and deeper into the same ideas and the same experiences.

As I describe in chapter 9, your integrated rule of life is a living, growing, strengthening organism that I encourage you to review and revise annually as you progress in your work and faith and move ever closer to achieving a solution to your chosen social struggle. The spiritual principles and practices you use to nurture an intimate, personal, and private relationship with God will likely increase, and those that you continue to use year after year will continuously mature your relationship with God. As you broaden your civic engagement, how you engage your spiritual principles and practices with those you work with and serve will mature and likely expand. Your desire to have a deeply committed and intimate relationship with God will be progressively fulfilled with each passing year. Your journal is the place to help you document this growth—maybe reviewing your journal is how you recognize your progress!

You may also want to read *The Way of the Urban Monk* as part of a group and use the reflection questions as points for conversation. Church book clubs may use the reflection questions as avenues for deepening faith. Social justice groups may read the book together as a way to welcome new members, foster unity, collectively deepen commitment, and replenish energy and inspiration. Educators may want to include this book in the curriculum for religion and public policy classes, urban studies, faith formation, or other appropriate studies.

My passion for this book is fueled by my desire to share with you my integrated rule of life, which I have continuously shaped over the past few decades and will continue to shape into a unique spiritual legacy. I find sharing—and ultimately bequeathing—my lifelong integrated rule of life to be a fulfillment of my personal living covenant with God, which will include my future efforts to integrate my spiritual principles and practices with my efforts to help right social wrongs. I hope my experiences will encourage you to shape and share your own integrated rule of life as a matchless spiritual legacy for others.

1

An Integrated Rule of Life

Your Map to Effective Spiritually Informed Social Justice

God places us in the world as his fellow workers-agents of transfiguration. We work with God so that injustice is transfigured into justice, so there will be more compassion and caring, that there will be more laughter and joy, that there will be more togetherness in God's world.

—Archbishop Desmond Tutu

Do your little bit of good where you are; it is those little bits of good put together that overwhelm the world.

—Archbishop Desmond Tutu

Urban monks are ordinary people who seek to live extraordinary lives by deepening a personal, living covenant with God as agents of change and healing in the communities in which they live, work, worship, recreate, socialize, and serve. They not only encounter the injustices experienced by others but seek to engage and end these injustices by furthering the teachings of Jesus Christ and the traditions of past and contemporary Christian reformers.

Anyone can become an urban monk by living out personally chosen spiritual principles and practices found in the Bible, integrated with efforts to find solutions for solving social struggles. Such spiritual principles and practices are usually taught by spiritual mentors only as a means to nurture an intimate, personal, and private relationship with God. Rarely are they taught as a means to nurture a deep, collective, and public relationship with God to help encounter, engage, and end social injustices. It is my mission to show how we can each create what I will refer to as the urban monk's "integrated rule of life."

My idea of an integrated rule of life was initially shaped by the Divine Office of Prayer, which I first encountered as a student at Notre Dame High School in Niles, Illinois. Drawing on the prayer book of the Holy Cross, the religious order of the priests that taught at the high school, we students were taught about the spiritual benefits of the everyday prayers, devotions, and reflections, and committing certain times of the day to reading the prayer book.

Each semester, juniors and seniors could choose how to spend the last hour of the school day; we could sign up for either a typing class or a study period. I always chose the study period, which took place in the school library—not to study but to read the daily newspaper, usually starting with the sports section, or to browse the magazine shelves. At times I would wander around the library, which of course had a religion section. It was there that I stumbled across a small, thin edition of the Rule of St. Benedict, a sixth-century text that lays out practical tools for living a Christ-centered life. Though originally written by Benedict of Nursia for cloistered monastic communities, this guide would later influence my thinking about what it means to live a Christ-centered, social justice-focused life outside the monastery—that is, what it means to be an urban monk.

In the traditional Christian sense, a rule of life is essentially a personal living covenant with God. Within the context of Christian theology, the word *covenant* principally refers to the solemn promises made between God and the Israelites in the Old Testament and between Christ and his followers in the New Testament. A biblical covenant is often based upon temporal and spiritual blessings and renewal. In an integrated rule of life, a covenant represents solemn promises and spiritual renewal between God and the individual. This includes not only nurturing a personal and private relationship with God, but *also* a relationship that is lived out in the secular community and moves beyond charitable acts into planned activities that seek to engage and end social injustices.

The spiritual principles and practices that form the foundation of an integrated rule of life and are found in the Christian Scriptures are rooted

An Integrated Rule of Life

in the passion of Jesus Christ. The source of Jesus's passion was his intense love for humanity, which resulted in his uncompromising commitment to restore humanity both spiritually and physically. Jesus expressed this love both privately with God and in community with his disciples. Like Jesus, an urban monk seeks to express an intense love for humanity by nurturing a private and public relationship with God and others. By "public relationship" I don't mean proselytizing, but rather employing spiritual principles and practices in the secular community—for example, serving on coalitions, committees, and councils committed to solving social struggles, and within local government—in an effort to find solutions for social injustice. In short, putting your spirituality in action to heal the world.

Creating an Integrated Rule of Life

An urban monk builds an integrated rule of life on biblically rooted spiritual principles and practices that can be found in the actions and writings of ancient and contemporary Christian mystics and reformers, such as St. Benedict, John Wesley, Desmond Tutu, and those who have learned from them. These mystics and reformers demonstrated an intimate relationship with God and an ability to integrate their spiritual principles and practices with social action. Consequently, they became agents of change and healing after confronting injustices and advocating to end them, thus furthering the teachings of Christ and their own tradition of Christian reform.

Urban monks can follow in this tradition by developing and practicing an integrated rule of life in three ways:

1. Nurturing an intimate, personal, and private relationship with God.
2. Carrying out acts of charity.
3. Committing to working with others to reverse the unjust conditions that make individual acts of charity necessary.

Nurturing an Intimate, Personal, and Private Relationship with God

Urban monks can learn how to cultivate an intimate, personal, and private relationship with God from several rules that have been practiced throughout the centuries by monastics. Some of the well-known rules include the rules of St. Benedict, St. Augustine, and the anonymous Master. Each of these rules provides instructions for monks to live a contemplative life, including spiritual practices such as prayer, chanting, Scripture reading, meditation, contemplation, silence, and fasting. For example, in the prologue to his rule, Benedict instructs, "Clothed then with faith and the performance of good works, let us set out on this way, with the Gospel as our guide, that we may deserve to see the Holy One 'who has called us to the eternal presence' (1 Thess 2:12). If we wish to dwell in God's tent, we will never arrive unless we run there by doing good deeds"; and, "First of all, every time you begin a good work, you must pray to God most earnestly to bring it to perfection."

Traditional rules also include appointed hours and days for these activities; acts of reverence during prayer—kneeling, bowing, or raising one's hands—and Scripture reading; and steps and stages of meditation, contemplation, and cultivating humility and obedience.

Urban monks can draw many of their spiritual practices from these rules to cultivate a personal relationship with God. While the rules were intended to be used in traditional monastic communities, anyone seeking a contemplative way of life can use them as a guide to integrate their principles and practices into their daily life outside of a shared community.

Carrying Out Acts of Charity

Charity is generally defined as generosity and helpfulness, especially toward the needy or suffering. The ancient rules of life emphasize acts of charity, particularly distributing one's possessions to the poor. Hospitality is to be shown to those inside and outside the monastery. Visitors to the monastery should be welcomed as if they were Christ and given food, clothing, and a warm place to sleep. The Rule of the Master, an early sixth-century rule written by an anonymous abbot, encourages monastics to take a little extra food and drink with them for those who need nourishment when they go out in public. Chapter 4 of the Rule of St. Benedict contains a list of good works that encourage monastics not to forsake charity and to comfort the poor, clothe the naked, and visit the sick.

Such acts of charity are in accordance with the parable of the sheep and goats found in Matthew 25:31–46—possibly one of the most well-known passages in the Bible—where Christ proclaims that when he comes in his glory, he will separate the nations into two groups: one that has responded to the needs of others and another group that has not. To the righteous he will say,

> "For I was hungry and you gave me something to eat, I was thirsty and you gave me something to drink, I was a stranger and you invited me in, I needed clothes and you clothed me, I was sick and you looked after me, I was in prison and you came to visit me."
>
> Then the righteous will answer him, "Lord, when did we see you hungry and feed you, or thirsty and give you something to drink? When did we see you a stranger and invite you in, or needing clothes and clothe you? When did we see you sick or in prison and go to visit you?" The King will reply, "Truly I tell you, whatever you did for one of the least of these brothers and sisters of mine, you did for me." (Matt 25:35–40)

James 2:14–17 also supports such acts of charity. After emphasizing that those who "love their neighbors as themselves" (Jas 2:8) are those who will inherit God's kingdom, James states,

> What good is it, my brothers and sisters, if someone claims to have faith but has no deeds? Can such faith save them? Suppose a brother or a sister is without clothes and daily food. If one of you says to them, "Go in peace; keep warm and well fed," but does nothing about their physical needs, what good is it? In the same way, faith by itself, if it is not accompanied by action, is dead. (Jas 2:14–17)

Later in the same chapter, after noting how the Old Testament figures Abraham and Rahab linked their faith with their actions, the author of the book of James underscores this point: "As the body without the spirit is dead, so faith without deeds is dead" (Jas 2:26). Similarly, in the first of his epistles, the apostle John, after noting the intensity of Christ's love for humanity, emphatically states,

> If anyone has material possessions and sees a brother or sister in need but has no pity on them, how can the love of God be in that person? Dear children, let us not love with words or speech but with actions and in truth. (1 John 3:17–18)

Carrying out such acts of charity can be characterized as expressing kindness that flows out of a state of abundance in terms of money, time, or talent. For example, we may give spare money to a homeless person on the street or to a charitable organization that serves the poor. Or we may volunteer to serve meals at a homeless shelter. The urban monk would do well to follow John Wesley's guidance: "Do all the good you can, by all the means you can, in all the ways you can, in all the places you can, at all the times you can, to all the people you can, as long as ever you can."

Committing to Working for Justice

Acts of charity are supportive—and perhaps even lifesaving at times—but they do little to address the underlying factors that contribute to conditions such as poverty and homelessness. Thus, they become the necessary bandage covering the unjust reality that surrounds people in need. Throughout the centuries, countless religious orders, charitable organizations, and individuals have tried to make up for large-scale injustices through acts of charity. Unfortunately, such efforts cannot end pervasive injustices unless such charitable acts are interwoven with demands on the practices and systems that create and perpetuate the injustices. The reality is that too few organizations and individuals link acts of charity with demands for justice.

For an urban monk, charity and justice are two sides of the same coin. Charitable acts should not end with meeting a person's immediate needs. A sequence of activities should follow that aims to end the injustices at the root of their suffering and the suffering of others in similar circumstances. For example, many programs offer meals to people experiencing homelessness. While these programs may provide temporary relief from hunger, they do not address the root causes of homelessness as evidenced by the fact that many who participate in such programs continue to experience homelessness. To help solve the injustice, food programs should be accompanied by supportive services, including case management, to help end a person's homelessness experience.

Systemic change requires going beyond individual contributions of spare time, money, or talent. The apostle Luke told us that much will be expected from those to whom much has been given, and more will be demanded from those to whom much has been entrusted (Luke 12:48). Justice often requires individuals—and organizations such as congregations—to band together with others in collaborative, synergistic, and scalable ways. Individual acts of charity without collective efforts to create more just systems will never be able to reach all who are experiencing the same injustice.

God is a lover of justice, as written in the book of Psalms, and expects us to be the same. The psalmist states that "the LORD loves the just" (Ps 37:28a), which echoes God's proclamation "For I the LORD love justice" (Isa 61:8a). The psalmist makes it clear that justice is at the core of God's identity. Psalm 99:4 declares, "The King is mighty, he loves justice, you have established equity," and Psalm 89:14 notes that "righteousness and justice are the foundation of [God's] throne."

The psalms frequently refer to God administering justice for those in need, including the oppressed (9:9; 10:12; 103:6; 146:7); orphans (10:17; 68:5; 82:3; 146:9); the poor (12:5; 41:1; 72:4, 12; 140:12); the needy (12:5; 72:4, 12; 82:4; 109:31; 140:12); widows (68:5; 146:9); the desolate (68:6; 82:3); the weak (72:12; 82:3); the hungry (107:9; 146:7); and the brokenhearted (147:3).

The prophet Isaiah makes it clear that we are to administer justice on behalf of God: "This is what the LORD says," he proclaimed. "Maintain justice and do what is right, for my salvation is close at hand and my righteousness will soon be revealed" (Isa 56:1). Isaiah also declared, "Hear me, you heavens! Listen, earth! For the LORD has spoken" (Isa 1:2). "Learn to do right; seek justice. Defend the oppressed. Take up the cause of the fatherless; plead the case of the widow" (Isa 1:17).

One of my favorite verses in the book of Isaiah is 42:1, which I have personalized as part of my integrated rule of life through the practice of lectio divina (divine reading), which I will discuss in later chapters. Verse 1 is understood as a prophecy that was fulfilled by Christ, as noted in the Gospels during Christ's baptism by John the Baptist. I personalize the verse by inserting myself as the servant and reading the verse as God saying to me,

> Here is my servant, whom I uphold, my chosen in whom I delight; I have put my Spirit on him, and he will bring justice to the nations.

And I respond in dialogue with God by saying,

> I am your servant, whom you uphold, and your chosen in whom your soul delights. You have put your Spirit upon me and I will bring forth justice to the nations.

Two other favorite verses are found in a song of praise in Isaiah 26:8–9:

> "In the path of your judgments, O LORD, we have placed hope; your name and your renown are the soul's desire. My soul yearns for you in the night; my spirit within me earnestly seeks you. For when your judgments are in the earth, the inhabitants of the world learn righteousness."

I personalize the verses by praying, "My soul yearns for you, O God, in the night" and "My spirit longs for you in the morning when people learn your righteousness and when they walk in your just ways."

When I include the word *righteousness* in my prayer, I think of my fellow urban monks, past and present, who are committed to ending social injustices, because the Hebrew term *tzedek* means "righteousness, justice, or fairness."[1] *Tzedek* is a different concept from charity, which suggests benevolence and generosity as a result of an abundance of money, time, or talent. *Tzedek* is rooted in the concept of what is right and just. It is an act of righteousness steeped in justice. *Tzedakah*, which is taken from the word *tzedek*, refers to a religious obligation to do what is right and just. The renowned medieval rabbi, philosopher, and physician Moses Maimonides believed that the highest form of *tzedakah* was to give a gift, loan, or partnership that would result in recipients supporting themselves instead of living on the continuous charitable acts of others.[2]

Archbishop Desmond Tutu provides a stellar example of elevating his efforts for justice beyond charity by working in community with others. He dedicated his life and work to ending apartheid in South Africa. As an Anglican cleric and bishop, he could have contained his efforts to his faith community, but he sought to expand his reach for justice. He became the first black General Secretary of the South African Council of Churches, then helped form the United Democratic Front—a multiracial coalition of churches, civic associations, trade unions, and sports and student organizations unified in ending racism and apartheid. In time it grew to over three million members to become one of the most successful anti-apartheid organizations in South Africa. Archbishop Tutu also served as the chair of the Truth and Reconciliation Commission in South Africa, which focused on investigating the human rights violations that occurred from 1960 to 1994.[3]

Getting Started

The way of an urban monk involves creating and cultivating an integrated rule of life that includes all three elements—(1) nurturing an intimate, personal, and private relationship with God; (2) extending charity to others;

---

1. "Tzedakah: Charity," para 4.
2. "Tzedakah: Charity" para 4.
3. "International Civil Rights Walk of Fame: Desmond Tutu"; "Truth Commission: South Africa."

and (3) moving beyond individual acts of charity to publicly engage in community efforts to achieve justice and right social wrongs. In the pages ahead I will offer you information, ideas, and practical examples for designing your own rule of life. I will guide you through choosing the primary focus of your social justice endeavors, identifying the spiritual principles that will inform and fortify your efforts, and selecting the spiritual practices that will help sustain your commitment to social justice work and deepen your relationships with those you work with and for, as well as with God. I also provide reflection questions to help you personalize and internalize each aspect of your rule of life. You can contemplate these questions on your own in quiet reflection and/or in a journal, or you might want to discuss them within a group.

Reflection Questions

- What are some ways you might integrate and nurture your intimate, personal, and private relationship with God within your community?
- How might you apply your love of God to help find solutions to social injustice?
- What acts of charity do you carry out on a regular basis and what have they accomplished?
- How can you link your acts of charity with demands for justice to right social wrongs?

2

Choosing Your Social Struggle

> Do not be daunted immediately by fear and run away from the road that leads to salvation. It is bound to be narrow at the outset. But as we progress in this way of life and in faith, we shall run on the path of God's commandments, our hearts overflowing with the inexpressible delight of love.
>
> —St. Benedict, Prologue 48–49

URBAN MONKS ARE COMMITTED to solving, with others, local social injustices in the communities and cities in which they live, work, worship, recreate, socialize, and serve. As they encounter and engage these social struggles with the goal of ending them, they infuse their actions with their Christian faith and spiritual principles and practices. They may also commit to solving social struggles in the larger regions and countries in which their communities and cities reside.

One of the first steps in becoming an urban monk and designing your integrated rule of life is to choose the social struggles that you want to help solve with others. No city or town in the United States is untouched by social injustice of some kind: child abuse, racism and inequality, healthcare disparity, homelessness, human trafficking, hunger. Other social injustices may involve animal rights/welfare, climate change, crime, education, substance abuse, and unemployment. To try to tackle all of these at once would be impossible—no one person has the time, energy, and resources. So where do you begin? How do you begin?

Finding Your Focus

When committing to becoming an urban monk, it is helpful to decide on *one primary focus*—one area of social injustice in which you will devote most of your efforts. Why? The well-known advice about digging a well comes to mind: you won't find water by quickly digging a bunch of shallow holes. You have to stay put and dig deep to yield results.

Social justice work is a lot like digging a well. In most cases, there is no quick and easy fix. Problems like homelessness and inequality are complex. It takes time to understand the nuances of such issues, to learn the tools available for enacting change, and to become familiar with the networks of people and resources to tap in order to make progress. Committing to one primary focus allows urban monks to immerse themselves—to dig deep—in the world of their struggle.

Such a commitment is similar to the "vow of stability" in Benedict's rule. As the writer Lynne Baab explains, "To a monk or sister, [the vow of stability] means being committed to stay in this particular monastic house with these particular people. It means being willing to look for God here in the constancy of this place in this rhythm of life, rather than seeking God in ever-changing places and varied routines."[1]

Stability is especially important for the urban monk trying to solve a social injustice because of the inherent challenge in doing so. Taking a vow of stability—that is, making a commitment to one primary area of social injustice—means you're less likely to cut and run when the going gets tough, when it feels like you're not making any headway, when the problem seems insurmountable and the suffering too much to bear.

I began my involvement in homelessness in 1987 as a social worker for the City of Pasadena's Bad Weather Shelter. During December 1986 and January 1987, several homeless people died sleeping overnight at various outdoor locations in Los Angeles County, prompting a public outcry. Several temporary winter shelters were established to provide overnight shelter and meals. I helped to establish one of the winter shelters in Pasadena and was hired to supervise it during its first year of operation.

---

1. Baab, "Benedictine Spirituality."

The Bad Weather Shelter ran from late January through mid-March and did not have any entry requirements other than to follow basic health and safety rules. Each night the shelter was occupied by more than one hundred people, many of whom had chronic health problems, mental illness, and/or substance abuse issues. Many of them had been rejected by year-round shelters because they were unwilling to abide by the shelter rules, which included curfews, money management, drug and alcohol abstinence, substance abuse treatment, and regular meetings with a case manager to ensure compliance with these rules. Others who came to the shelter had been released earlier that same day from jail, foster care, hospitals, or mental health facilities and had nowhere else to go. Some were fleeing domestic violence and a few were fleeing from prostitution after being physically abused and traumatized by partners and pimps.

During the first year, I worked four twelve-hour shifts per week, during which I had to stay up all night. My duties included arriving in the early evening to let in a line of people and a few volunteers. We would set up cots, pass out blankets, and make a meal out of donated foods. After the meal, people would line up to shower.

During the night, I would stay up and observe the residents. There were always a few people moving about. Some of them would use the bathroom, others would step outside the front door to smoke, and others would sit in the dining area having another cup of coffee or eating leftovers. By the middle of the night, nearly everyone was finally asleep.

During this time, I would reflect on these experiences. One of the things that became evident was the intensity of the physical and emotional wounds of so many people in one place. During the previous two years, I had worked part-time as a case manager for a growing number of homeless people during the day. I did not see them at night. I realized that in the daytime I could work on ways to alleviate their pain. In the middle of the night, at the shelter, I could only wait and observe.

I could see the wounds and pains within the shelter intensify and culminate in this mass of deeply hurt individuals. Many of them were using alcohol or some other drug to deal with their homeless experience. They were the ones who were first in line to get in. Their drug consumption barely masked the pain they were trying to relieve. I concluded that they comprised about one-third of people who came each night to use the shelter. The shelter policy was that if you weren't rowdy, you stayed; if you were rowdy, you needed to leave and come back when you were not.

About one-third of the other shelter users were mentally ill. Very few of them got in line. They would wait until the line went down before coming into the shelter. Some were paranoid, and others deeply depressed. Others demonstrated psychotic behaviors, flailing their arms, muttering to themselves, or pacing the floor repeatedly. A few self-medicated by consuming alcohol or drugs.

The final third of shelter users were neither substance abusers nor mentally ill. Some were victims of domestic violence, often bringing children into the shelter. Because of the children, we separated these folks into a designated sleeping area. I often feared that the batterers would show up.

One incident is forever etched into my mind—watching a taxicab pull up in front of the shelter and seeing the driver get out, open the trunk, pull out a wheelchair, and unfold it. He went to the side door of the cab, opened it, then carried out a man who was clothed in a bathrobe and had no legs. The driver placed him in the wheelchair and rolled him into the shelter, where we helped him get something to eat and a place to sleep.

I remained the supervisor of the winter shelter in Pasadena for the following eight years. When the shelter season was extended to December through March, we hired other staff. A growing number of volunteers would set up the cots, pass out blankets, and prepare and serve meals. Evening staff would conduct an intake with every shelter resident, and other staff would stay overnight.

I stayed overnight fewer and fewer nights. I carried out my duties during the evenings with the goal of ensuring they were completed before I left. I was the common denominator, the one who had shaped the program and the one most familiar to staff, volunteers, and shelter residents.

Each evening, I went home to the small one-bedroom apartment where I lived alone. As soon as I arrived home, I would sit on my living room couch, staring at a blank television and reflecting on the evening's activities and the collective suffering I had witnessed. The more I reflected, the more deeply I shared the pain of the shelter residents. To cope with this nightly experience, I began to turn to some of the books that I had accumulated over the years, including *Christian Mysticism Today* by William Johnston. His conclusion to chapter 6 resonated profoundly with my progressive Catholic upbringing:

> The inward journey can be described as a journey into the depths of one's being, a journey to the true self and through the true self to God, who is at the center. Down, down, I go through alternate

layers of light and darkness, meeting all the slimy monsters and frightening demons that inhabit the subliminal world. And if I progress far enough, I meet the monsters of the human race. I meet the root causes of war, oppression, torture, hunger, terrorism. I meet hatred, despair, injustice, atheism, darkness, I meet archetypal evil. And, horror of horrors, I meet it in myself. In myself you say, how can that be? How can I be responsible for massacres of innocent people, for torture, for oppression of the poor? Alas, we are all responsible. For we all share in the collective acts of the human family. We are not isolated individuals but members of a living and conscious body.

Johnston concludes the chapter, "Most of us are not in touch with this collective unconscious. We are far too superficial for that." He notes that instead of pointing an accusing finger at others, we should "enter the world of politics or economics or law or whatever," noting that our influence in such spheres is crucial. He also states, "Others help the destitute poor or the underprivileged or the handicapped," which resonated with me. I began to sense that the city was becoming my monastery—a place where I was becoming increasingly willing to engage community development, economics, legislation, and politics, and to integrate my spiritual principles and practices with these efforts.

While it makes sense to choose one area of focus, it is not always easy to do so. With one look at the daily news it becomes clear that social injustice is pervasive. Of course we want to end all suffering, not just the suffering of the homeless or the hungry or those who are discriminated against. It's important to realize that even though you are choosing one primary focus, your efforts do not exist in vacuum. The headway you make in your chosen area of focus will certainly encourage positive change in other areas. For example, helping to solve local homelessness will likely involve dealing with several other issues that cause homelessness, such as a lack of affordable housing and health care, as well as mental illness, substance use, unemployment, and underemployment.

As you seek to determine your primary focus, you may begin with a social struggle that personally impacts you or those close to you: family members, friends, classmates, and coworkers. Below I look at a few other areas to mine for ideas.

Look to Your Education—Formal and Not

Many of us were exposed to the call to social justice somewhere in our education. When choosing your "monastery," it can help to reflect on those years to recall areas that especially spoke to your mind and heart. Maybe you first learned about the Catholic social justice icon Dorothy Day in primary school, and you remember being particularly moved reading about her tireless efforts to lift up the poorest members of society and establish the Catholic Worker Movement. Maybe you read some of the social consciousness writings of Charles Dickens about the poor and their children, such as *Oliver Twist*, which exposed the cruel treatment of orphans, and *Little Dorrit*, which revealed the horrific effects of debtor's prisons on parents and children.

Perhaps in high school you volunteered at a shelter for victims of domestic violence as part of a civics community outreach program and you recall feeling energized at the end of each shift because you made a difference. Maybe you remember finding a deeper level of theological reflection on racism after you were exposed to the writings of Thomas Merton in your college years. Perhaps the same was true upon reading how Booker T. Washington mobilized a nationwide network of pioneers, preachers, philanthropists, and politicians to achieve his goal to improve race relations. Mine the memories of your education for areas of interest and inspiration.

I was first inspired to encounter social injustices while in high school. The Catholic grade school and high school I graduated from was steeped in Catholic social teaching, which emphasized God's love for the poor and God's call to be a lover of justice. Through my high school education, I was taught by the words and convictions of ancient philosophers, Old Testament prophets, and Christ to stand up for the poor.

You don't need to have had a formal education to find direction in your urban monk efforts. Often the experiences we have in the proverbial "school of hard knocks" become the classroom in which wisdom is imparted. The key is to engage the world with a curious mind and every day becomes our teacher.

Over the years, I have always appreciated learning new things, and I looked to every person and experience as potential sources of discovery. Upon doing so there has always been the inclination to share such things with others. When it came to learning new things about peace and justice issues, I felt more urgency to share. I felt like a young monk who wanted to begin a spiritual reformation, or a young person who wanted to reclaim a social issue, such as affordable housing or homelessness, for a county or city.

Look to Your Social Heroes—Living or Legacy

Another area that can help us home in on a specific area of social justice is to look to our heroes. We all have people—living or from the past—whom we look up to as examples of individuals bettering our world. We may read their writings, hear their speeches, or benefit from their good works directly, and from there find our passion and motivation to enact change in our communities.

I first heard the following words credited to the Greek mathematician and inventor Archimedes while in high school: "Give me a place to stand and with a lever I will move the world." It was not until I became a young adult and was pursuing my bachelor's degree that I wanted to stand up for the poor. I found myself often quoting Archimedes to my friends and fellow students. However, I left out the words "with a lever." I was so inspired by the words "give me a place to stand" and "I will move the world" that "with a lever" did not seem to fit.

I was furthered inspired to assert "give me a place to stand and I will move the whole world" after I learned that the reformer Robert F. Kennedy, whose words have often inspired me, also left out "with a lever" when he quoted Archimedes after declaring,

> A young monk began the Protestant Reformation, a young general extended an empire from Macedonia to the borders of the earth, and a young woman reclaimed the territory of France. It was a young Italian explorer who discovered the New World, and the thirty-two-year-old Thomas Jefferson who proclaimed that all men are created equal.

Kennedy continued:

> "Give me a place to stand," said Archimedes, "and I will move the world." These [people] moved the world, and so can we all.

What may have added to my inspiration of this rendering was that my Roman Catholic grandparents, parents, uncles, and aunts admired Robert F. Kennedy. What Roman Catholic would not admire a person who declared that it was his Catholicism that gave him the strength to re-enter politics after the assassination of his older brother, John? Further adding to the inspiration I found in Kennedy's words was that I always liked to think of myself as an Italian-Sicilian explorer ready to discover new worlds.

Robert Kennedy's other brother, the US Senator Ted Kennedy, recited the full quote of Archimedes during a commencement speech over a decade ago. After asserting "If you give me a lever and a place to stand, I can move the world," he added, "Your excellent education here has given you that lever, and I hope that you will use it to move our country to address the many challenges we face more effectively."

To this day, I feel inspired when I read these words. A lever can be an object used with an appropriate pivot point to multiply the force or effort that can be applied to resistance force. A lever is also an object that can increase the distance and speed at which a resistance force travels. Within the context of peace and social justice issues, there are many experiences that can make us a lever, applied to a resistance force to effect positive societal change and increase the distance and speed at which that resistance force travels.

Look for Inspiration in Everyday Life

Where have you seen or felt compassion? Answering this question may help you narrow your focus on a specific social injustice where you can commit your urban monk efforts. Compassion generally grows out of allowing the hurts and pains of others to impact us and mature us, particularly if we deal with our own hurtful and painful experiences as a result. The Dutch-born Catholic priest Henri J. M. Nouwen describes such a person as being a "wounded healer."

The wounded healer was evident when Robert F. Kennedy quoted another ancient Greek, Aeschylus, during his speech on the night of the assassination of Martin Luther King Jr. After noting that he had also suffered through the assassination of his own brother, Kennedy declared that Aeschylus once wrote, "Even in our sleep, pain which cannot forget falls drop by drop upon the heart, until in our own despair, against our will, comes wisdom through the awful grace of God."

Kennedy followed the quote with the following words:

> What we need in the United States is not division; what we need in the United States is not hatred; what we need in the United States is not violence or lawlessness; but love and wisdom, and compassion toward one another, and a feeling of justice toward those who

still suffer within our country, whether they be white or they be black. . . . Let us dedicate ourselves to what the Greeks wrote so many years ago: to tame the savageness of man and make gentle the life of this world.

I will explore the concept of the wounded healer as a practice in a later chapter.

Look to the Work That Makes You Feel Purposeful, Satisfied, of Service

Engaging a social injustice will likely be a gradual experience, and may begin with acts of charity. As you go about your work, pay attention to when you feel most energized, purposeful, and satisfied with your efforts. When do you feel most of service?

When I chose local homelessness as the social wrong that I wanted to right, my initial engagement involved acts of charity. I donated food and served meals at a local homeless shelter. I soon became involved with coalitions, committees, and commissions that conducted public meetings during which concerns about homelessness were discussed to help develop a local understanding of the issues that led to homelessness, as well as to explore how to respond to homelessness.

Homeless counts soon furthered my involvement with trying to solve local homelessness with others in Pasadena, where I lived and worked. The US Census Bureau made a significant effort to enumerate homelessness at the national level, which was referred to as "S-Night." (The "S" stood for both a street and shelter count.) The effort introduced the notion of enumerating homelessness in every community and city.

The US Census Bureau soon released its homeless numbers by jurisdiction, including Pasadena, which was 439 homeless persons. Of the 439 persons, 234 were counted as unsheltered and 205 as sheltered.

Many of us trying to solve local homelessness knew this number was too low. I led the effort to conduct a local homeless count that took place on September 23, 1992. We divided the city into sixteen zones and a team of volunteer counters was assigned to each zone. The total count was 1,017 homeless adults and children.

Not only did volunteers count each person, but they also asked each adult approximately thirty survey questions to help shape a homeless strategy with recommendations to prevent and end local homelessness.

Questions regarding basic demographics (age, ethnicity, gender, and race) were included as well as questions that focused on health, income, mental health, and substance use.

A Homeless Count Advisory Committee was created to decide what questions would be included in the survey. The committee was also charged with making sure the committee recruited a range of volunteer counters from public and private entities. Representatives included city officials and staff from such departments as Human Services, Housing and Development, Planning, Building and Neighborhood Services, and the Accessibility and Disability Commission, as well as school district representatives, business and neighborhood association members, members of the homeless community, and several homeless service providers who provided health, mental health, and substance use services.

A similar homeless count and survey was conducted every two years afterward, and the data was used to update the homeless strategy and recommendations to help solve local homelessness. The count and survey helped reverse a trend of aversion and avoidance of homeless people. One of the more surprising findings was the number of homeless children. The first count and survey in 1992 revealed that 203—20 percent of the people counted—were children; 117 of the 203 children were under five years of age, and 63 of them were two years old or younger.

In 2005, the US Department of Housing and Urban Development (HUD) began requiring jurisdictions to conduct a sheltered and unsheltered count and survey to help shape a federal plan to prevent and end homelessness. The data was also to be used to inform homeless strategies at a local level. Pasadena has continued to conduct a sheltered and unsheltered count and survey every year.

Your Place to Stand

Helping to end a social injustice can only happen after encountering and engaging the social injustice with others doing the same.

For me, finding my place to stand so I could move the world began with designing and implementing homeless counts and surveys. Encountering homeless people on the streets stirred in me the desire for a place to stand so I could move the world; especially upon engaging them through acts of charity. But I truly found my footing after becoming publicly involved with other people who wanted to prevent and end local homelessness. I began to stand tall, and I felt that I could start to move the world of local homelessness through homeless counts and surveys, beginning with Pasadena. Over the years, I have helped many cities and counties throughout Southern California complete homeless counts and surveys to meet HUD's requirements and gather local information.

My gradual experience of working to end a social injustice—local homelessness—evolved when I began to help local jurisdictions craft and implement homelessness strategies. The findings based on count and survey data collected over the years were compared, revealing data trends. These trends were shared with various stakeholders—including local coalitions, committees, and commissions—to help shape recommendations. Until data trends were shared, the public's desire to help homeless people far exceeded its knowledge about homelessness.

My experience of helping to end homelessness also evolved when I was able to help develop nonresidential programs that implemented local recommendations by promoting street outreach teams and street medicine, including health care, mental health care, and substance use recovery. I also helped develop several residential programs to implement local recommendations, including temporary housing, such as shelters, and transitional housing to help ready residents obtain permanent housing. These programs also included permanent supportive housing, which provides support services and case management to residents so they can maintain their housing and not return to homelessness.

What really helped me feel like I had a place to stand tall and move the world was helping to write grants to fund nonresidential and residential programs. I have helped write grants for many jurisdictions throughout California over the years. These grants ranged from tens of thousands to tens of millions of dollars.

During the past twenty-five years, I have completed several "Impediments to Fair Housing Choice" reports, which are required by HUD from local jurisdictions that receive HUD funding. The purpose of the reports is to review the local jurisdiction's laws and regulations, along with its administrative policies, procedures, and practices, to ensure that residents are not denied access to housing based upon such factors as race, color, religion, sex, disability, familial status, income, or national origin. Based on our research and reporting, I was able to help get several jurisdictions to change their laws, policies, and practices to ensure that homeless people were not discriminated against when obtaining appropriate housing.

Choosing Your Social Struggle

I have helped local jurisdictions focus on homeless people languishing on the streets with life-threatening illnesses, with terminal illnesses, and while aging with such illnesses. I have also helped look more closely at infant mortality among the homeless.

Your journey as an urban monk will involve a long-term commitment to a course of action that leads to helping others implement solutions to end your primary social struggle and related social injustices. There's no question that the problems are big and complex, and long-term solutions can seem elusive. But as your integrated rule of life evolves, so will your confidence that these seemingly intractable social struggles can be resolved.

Reflection Questions

- In what ways were you exposed to the call to social justice growing up? A book? A class? A lecture? A volunteer opportunity?
- Describe the social struggle that has personally impacted you or those close to you—family, friends, classmates, coworkers—the most?
- How might you find a place to stand tall with others within the efforts to solve a social struggle that has collectively impacted you?

3

Spiritual Principles

Discerning the Values That Will Light Your Way

> We want spiritual principles to be more than beautiful abstractions; we want them to actually transform our lives.
>
> —Marianne Williamson

SPIRITUAL PRINCIPLES ARE VALUES taught by the world's spiritual traditions throughout the centuries that can help us as we influence, implement, infer, and innovate solutions to right social wrongs. The leadership authority and bestselling author Stephen Covey defines principles as

> deep fundamental truths, classic truths, generic common denominators. They are tightly interwoven threads running with exactness, consistency, beauty and strength through the fabric of life. . . . We can be secure in the knowledge that principles are bigger than people or circumstances, and that thousands of years of history have seen them triumph, time and time again. Even more important, we can be secure in the knowledge that we can validate them in our own lives, by our own experience.[1]

In Christianity, these values include faith, hope, love, forgiveness, acceptance, reconciliation, humility, integrity, honor, service, grace, and discernment.

---

1. Covey, *7 Habits of Highly Effective People*, 122–23.

Spiritual Principles

Spiritual principles, a foundational building block for any integrated rule of life, deepen our understanding of social wrongs and spur and sustain our courage and commitment to right the wrongs as we cultivate them over time. For example, your faith, hope, and love will likely deepen with each social struggle you engage with others. Forgiveness, acceptance, and reconciliation will deepen when you encounter the hurt and pain of others. Humility, integrity, honor, service, and grace will deepen as you get closer with others working together to right a social wrong. Others will see your actions aligning with your words, which you will want to reinforce.

How do you as an urban monk identify the spiritual principles that will factor into your rule of life? It's a personal choice, achieved through discernment and reflecting upon your relationship with God. You may initially include two or three spiritual principles and add others as you become more involved in solving your chosen social struggle. The list may evolve as you mature in your knowledge and civic actions to solve social injustices and as your relationship with God deepens.

When I first became involved with homelessness, I was a volunteer serving food to homeless people. I wanted to faithfully believe that the problem could be solved, but I hoped to overcome my lingering doubts as I learned to love my homeless neighbor as myself. I soon became more involved by participating in community meetings where seemingly irreconcilable positions, including my own, had to be reconciled through mutual forgiveness, acceptance, and reconciliation. The more publicly involved I became, the more I realized I needed to proceed with humility, integrity, honor, grace, and service to build and fortify trusting relationships with those I was working with to solve social issues and injustices.

A Closer Look at Core Spiritual Principles

Below I look at some core Christian spiritual principles and show how they may guide and fortify you specifically in your efforts to solve social injustice. The list can help you begin to examine yourself as you design your integrated rule of life.

Faith

When working to advance solutions to social injustices, we will inevitably ask, "Can we really solve this problem?" The theologian Paul Tillich proclaimed that "doubt is not the opposite of faith; it is one element of faith." Thus, doubt can become a catalyst for growth in your faith that solutions to social struggles can be achieved.

I doubt that homelessness will ever end. However, my faith is a spiritual principle that I integrated into my rule of life as I became more involved in alleviating homelessness. I soon realized that though homelessness will never end, homelessness can end for an individual, a family, or many people living in an encampment. I can attest that over the past couple of decades, my involvement with homelessness has helped hundreds of people end homelessness for thousands of people who were languishing on the streets.

The writer of the book of Hebrews provides a definition of faith that ultimately helps us overcome our doubts: "Now faith is confidence in what we hope for and assurance about what we do not see. This is what the ancients were commended for" (Heb 11:1–2).

Hope

The Catholic social activist Catherine de Hueck Doherty said, "Faith walks simply, childlike, between the darkness of human life and the hope of what's to come." As one's faith grows, so can one's hope, which is key to community and civic involvement. Hope fosters positive expectations and outcomes. Even the slightest progress to solve social struggles can cultivate hope, and that hope empowers us to take further steps in our work to right social wrongs. Thus, faith and hope are prerequisites for sustaining the work of the urban monk.

Hope also helps us overcome doubts about whether we can solve complex and pervasive social issues. While hope implies little certainty, it infers confidence and conviction in the possibility of a solution. As we read in Ephesians 2:10, "For we are God's handiwork, created in Christ Jesus to do good works, which God prepared in advance for us to do."

The theologian Henri Nouwen believed that "hope is based on the premise that the other gives only what is good. Hope includes an openness by which you wait for the promise to come through, even though you never know when, where, or how this might happen." I can think back to when, where, and how my first feelings of hope evolved about ending homelessness.

My initial involvement with homeless people was as a volunteer passing out bowls of oatmeal to a long line of people who came to the counter for breakfast. At that time, I was struggling with my own stereotypes about people who were homeless, namely, that many of them were alcoholics, drug addicts, and mentally ill. The more I volunteered, the more I struggled with my misconceptions.

My struggle continued on the streets of Pasadena where I lived and worked. When I would walk the streets by myself or with friends, I increasingly recognized many of the people to whom I'd served breakfast, and they recognized me. Over time we were addressing each other by name. I can remember one person calling out to me by name, and I called out to him by his street name—Smokey. One time, in a park where there were a lot of homeless people, including Smokey, I went over to where he was sitting. He shouted out to everyone, "If you have a problem with Joe, you have a problem with me."

Memphis—he was from Memphis, Tennessee—was another guy I frequently saw while walking the streets. At first, I called him Marty, his real name. Other homeless people were surprised to hear me call him Marty. But he told them it was okay for me to call him by his first name. Another person I became familiar with was Pat. When I ran into her on the streets, she was usually alone, and we would stop and talk. Soon she told me I could call her by her Irish name, Paddy.

Smokey, Memphis, and Paddy initially honed my spiritual principles, particularly my sense of hope, that evolved as I engaged more and more homeless people. I did not know at first, though I hoped, that I would help end homelessness while working with hundreds of other people who desired the same. My hope grew each year, as did my faith, as I witnessed hundreds of people each year obtain and maintain permanent housing.

Love

In concluding his well-known passage on love in 1 Corinthians, Paul explains the hierarchy of these principles: "And now these three remain: faith, hope, and love; but the greatest of these is love" (1 Cor 13:13). In the Gospel of Mark, Jesus declares that the first and greatest commandment is to "love the Lord your God with all your heart and with all your soul and with all your mind." He then proclaims that "the second is this: 'Love your neighbor as yourself'" (Mark 12:30–31). These commandments are proof that an urban monk cannot design their integrated rule of life without love as a centerpiece. After all, as Mother Teresa wrote, "Not all of us can do great things. But we can so small things with great love."

Loving your neighbor as yourself is key for the urban monk moving from a more private notion of spirituality to a more publicly engaged one. Stepping up in civic engagement to support our social struggles means our ideas, opinions, and convictions—as well as our physical, emotional, and spiritual resources—will likely be challenged by naysayers, critics, and competing agendas. Christ's teachings about love can strengthen us to withstand the pressures of public service and guide our reactions: "Do to others as you would have them do to you" (Luke 6:31) and "Give to the one who asks you, and do not turn away from the one who wants to borrow from you" (Matt 5:42).

New Testament writers emphasize Christ's teachings by encouraging us to remember "the words the Lord Jesus himself said: 'It is more blessed to give than to receive'" (Acts 20:35) and that "love does no harm to a neighbor" (Rom 13:10).

I fulfill the second greatest commandment by referring to homeless people as my neighbors and helping others do the same. The idea is to humanize people experiencing homelessness, both in our planning meetings to solve this social issue and in our everyday conversations. In some of our committees, we refer to homeless people as our sisters and brothers, sometimes even as our mothers and fathers. As it reads in James 2:8, "If you really keep the royal law found in Scripture, 'Love your neighbor as yourself,' you are doing right."

Forgiveness

Forgiveness can prove to be one of the more challenging spiritual principles when working with others, but it may be needed between you and another because of past hurtful experiences or events. You may find forgiveness challenging, even if a past event did not involve you. Others you are working with may be struggling to let go of the hurt, ill will, or resentment they experienced due to an unresolved social struggle that has been negatively impacting them and/or family and friends. For example, someone who became homeless because of domestic violence may still be experiencing the negative effects of trauma and the fear of being retraumatized.

Jesus taught, "If someone slaps you on one cheek, turn to them the other also. If someone takes your coat, do not withhold your shirt from them" (Luke 6:29). Whether you are one who was stricken by hurt or anger or the one who inflicted it, whether intentionally or unintentionally, forgiveness is fundamental to working together to solve social struggles. As essential as it is, it is often not easy to achieve. As I explained earlier, the very social struggle you're working on may bring together those who were hurt in the past and those who contributed to causing the pain—those who feel unheard and those who are being accused of turning a deaf ear. A good example relating to homelessness is property owners. Rent control has often been a hot-button issue with property owners who do not want rent control and people who are at risk of losing their housing because of large rent increases. I have seen property owners show remorse regarding evictions and renters feeling shame when unable to pay their rent. Within the context of public engagement, forgiveness is not just about bringing healing to the past but well-being to the future. Forgiveness is a willingness to let go of aches and anger for a restored past and a recovering future.

Forgiveness is letting go of the hurt, ill will, and resentments that others have inflicted in the past—people, groups, or institutions who may now be participants in the group you are part of and who are working to right those wrongs. Working toward solving a social struggle will be easier if you ask for forgiveness for inflicting an injustice on a person or group of people, whether your action was intentional or not.

In my experience in working to end homelessness, engaging people with lived experience of homelessness has been one of the more challenging experiences concerning forgiveness for all involved. The US Department of Housing and Urban Development (HUD) and the US Interagency Council on Homelessness (USICH) strongly encouraged communities, cities, counties, and coalitions to engage people with lived experience of homelessness during public meetings. Their research showed that inviting people with lived experience into the process of solving the problems that affect or affected them leads to better crafted local solutions to prevent and end homelessness. So, we invited homeless people to attend our planning meetings, gave them opportunities to respond to the ideas generated in those meetings, and listened when they offered their own solutions. In our meetings, people experiencing homelessness emphasized the importance of trauma- and survivor-informed training for street outreach workers to help ensure workers provide access to appropriate supportive services and related resources.

In our public forums, people shared their traumatic experiences that were the result of violence, crime, and illnesses while languishing on the streets. They shared about the lasting effects of their trauma and how their fear of being retraumatized caused them to live in a constant state of survival rather than taking the steps necessary to get off the streets, as counterintuitive as it may seem. Their participation allowed them to express their pain and feel heard, which facilitated healing by helping them forgive others and be forgiven by others.

Many people who were working to end homelessness had never been homeless themselves and therefore never knew about the effects of trauma, nor how the fear of being retraumatized impacted people's efforts to end their homelessness. Communities comprising people with and without lived experience of homelessness are more effective in solving the problem because they have a greater understanding of it.

The spiritual principle of forgiveness inherently emphasizes the "integrated" in our integrated rule of life because it requires us to call on other spiritual principles, including love and faith. As the Dominican scholar Matthew Fox explains, "Forgiveness requires *some great love*, a love that beckons one to another horizon, another place, another relationship. Sometimes this call is clear, and sometimes it lurks in the dark, is muffled, and requires faith even to catch a faint echo of its presence."

Acceptance

Acceptance and self-acceptance are two sides of the same coin. Acceptance involves coming to terms with what a person, group of people, or an institution did to you, then letting go and moving on in the spirit of forgiveness. Self-acceptance involves coming to terms with yourself, realizing that you have to forgive to be forgiven, and that you have not only been afflicted with hurt but have also inflicted hurt upon others.

Acceptance is not about approving or condoning what needs to be forgiven. It is about mutual forgiveness and a reminder that all of us inflict hurt and pain. The teachings of Christ include "Forgive, and you will be forgiven" (Luke 6:37) and "Let any one of you who is without sin be the first to throw a stone" (John 8:7).

Acceptance and self-acceptance are essential to solving any social struggle. Holding on to ill will and resentment is both self-defeating and group-defeating. We can extend forgiveness to others whether they admit to inflicting harm or not. If they are holding on to ill will and resentment, our acceptance may be what helps them let go. As Katharine Jefferts Schori, the former presiding bishop and primate of the Episcopal Church of the United States, explains, "Those who know the deep acceptance and love that come with healing and forgiveness can lose the defensive veneer that wants to shut out other sinners."

Losing the defensive veneer is essential to solving a social struggle such as homelessness, and this often begins with accepting that we are *all* in need of some level of forgiveness. As Thomas Merton explains, when we share forgiveness, its healing effects can be self-perpetuating:

> We do not really know how to forgive until we know what it is to be forgiven. Therefore we should be glad that we can be forgiven by [others]. It is our forgiveness of one another that makes the love of Jesus for us manifest in our lives, for in forgiving one another we act towards one another as He has acted towards us.

By no means does forgiveness signify that you and others are accepting of the social struggle. As a matter of fact, losing the defensive veneer can lead to real progress. As the activist Angela Davis notes, "I *am no longer accepting* the things I cannot change. I *am* changing the things I cannot *accept*," which is essential for righting a social wrong.

Reconciliation

Reconciliation is not just a change but an *exchange*. It is not just about you understanding a social struggle differently. It is about being willing to exchange seemingly irreconcilable perceptions and positions—to see things from the perspective of others and to understand why they are taking their position on the social struggle.

The goal of this mutual exchange is to reconcile differing perceptions and positions to arrive at a collective solution to right a social wrong. Reconciliation requires you not only to realize but to support the actions of others—even those you feel are unnecessary or contrary to the solution you envision. And as Henri Nouwen explains, reconciliation asks us to put aside our judgments:

> In a world that constantly asks us to make up our minds about other people, a nonjudgmental presence seems nearly impossible.

But it is one of the most beautiful fruits of a deep spiritual life and will be easily recognized by those who long for reconciliation.[2]

The Scriptures tell us that "fools mock the making of amends for sin, but goodwill is found among the upright" (Prov 14:9). The Scriptures also tell us, "Trust in the Lord with all your heart, and lean not on your own understanding; in all your ways submit to him, and he will make your paths straight" (Prov 3:5–6).

Dealing with homeless encampments over the years has taught me that reconciliation is both transformation *and* relationship. While attending our planning meeting, some participants have pointed out that encampments become a health and safety hazard and a public nuisance, which is often true. Others will say that removing the encampment will only result in those people establishing an encampment elsewhere, which is also often true.

Over the years, public engagement has resulted in reconciling differing views into collective solutions that have been promoted by HUD and the USICH. Collective solutions include providing access to temporary and permanent housing options before removing the encampment, and afterward taking measures to provide security, prevent unsafe and unhealthful conditions, such as trash and fires, and encourage the use of the newly open space to prevent further encampments.

Humility

St. Bernard of Clairvaux was once asked, "What are the three most important aspects of the spiritual life?" He replied, "Humility, humility, humility."

Humility can become a dynamic force when shifting from a private notion of spirituality to a more public one. As a spiritual principle, humility is recognition of the self in relationship to God. The writer of the epistle to the Philippians urged,

> Do nothing out of selfish ambition or vain conceit. Rather, in humility value others above yourselves, not looking to your own interests but each of you to the interests of the others. In your relationships with one another, have the same mindset as Christ Jesus. (Phil 2:3–5)

---

2. Nouwen, *Bread for the Journey*, December 27.

Spiritual Principles

When we're passionate about solving a social issue, it is easy to feel wedded to our own convictions and designs for implementing change. Humility helps us get past our own egos, agendas, and ideas. It helps us listen better, understand more deeply, and share more collaboratively. Thinking of ourselves less and more about others is essential to affecting social change and to any integrated rule of life.

Joan D. Chittister reminds us of the second step of humility words of St. Benedict of Nursia, "Humility is that we love not our own will nor take pleasure in the satisfaction of our desires; rather we shall imitate by our actions that saying of Christ's: 'I have come not to do my own will but the will of the One who sent me' (John 6:38)."[3]

Integrity

People with integrity are the building blocks of effective, solution-oriented advocacy. Those who demonstrate integrity draw others into community engagement because they are seen as trustworthy and dependable. They are viewed as principled and can be counted on to act in admirable ways even when no one is aware of their activity.

Integrity is the foundation on which solutions to social struggles are built. Demonstrating integrity as an urban monk builds relationships, trust, and effective interactions among those who are engaged in the work of solving the social struggle. People generally respond well to those whose outward actions and service align with their words.

As Martin Luther King Jr. exclaimed,

> May I stress the need for courageous, intelligent, and dedicated leadership.... Leaders of sound integrity. Leaders not in love with publicity, but in love with justice. Leaders not in love with money, but in love with humanity. Leaders who can subject their particular egos to the greatness of the cause.[4]

King was deeply influenced by the integrity of his own father:

> I have rarely ever met a person more fearless and courageous than my father.... The thing that I admire most about my dad is his genuine Christian character. He is a man of real integrity,

---

3. Chittister, *The Rule of Benedict: Insight for the Ages*, 66.
4. King, "Desegregation and the Future," Address delivered at the Annual Luncheon of the National Committee for Rural Schools, para. 26.

deeply committed to moral and ethical principles. He is conscientious in all of his undertakings. . . . If I had a problem I could always call Daddy.[5]

Honor

Honor can forge a bond between you and those who seek to solve a social struggle. The abolitionist and poet Ralph Waldo Emerson believed that the purpose of life "is to be useful, to be honorable, to be compassionate, to have it make some difference that you have lived and lived well."[6]

Honor can manifest as a code of conduct that involves keeping your word, which means you will do what you say or promise. You will follow through with actions that will fulfill what you said or promised. Like integrity, demonstrating honor as an urban monk builds trusting relationships with those whom you are working alongside to solve social injustices. When we act honorably, others will respond well to our actions.

Honor can also manifest when we accept personal responsibility. We must be prepared to accept the consequences of our actions. Knowing what is right is not as important as doing what is right. We must follow the spirit as well as the letter of the law.

Hebrews 13:18 encourages us to "desire to live honorably in every way," and 1 Peter 2:12 urges us to conduct ourselves with such honor that others "may see (our) good deeds and glorify God" because, as Romans 14:18 states, "anyone who serves Christ in this way is pleasing to God and receives human approval."

Service

As a spiritual principle, service means being intentional about ameliorating a negative situation. It takes the form of helping others or a cause to improve a condition by volunteering one's time and energy, either as a one-time commitment or on an ongoing basis. Service can be our contribution—individually or as part of a collective—to the efforts of a group of friends, a club, a community agency, or an entire city or county. The

---

5 King, *The Autobiography of Martin Luther King Jr.*, 4–5.
6 Excellence Reporter, "Ralph Waldo Emerson," para. 1.

spiritual principle of service also expresses obedience to God by helping people in God's name.

The Scriptures are filled with divine directives to help those who are in need, whether elderly, homeless, hungry, infirm, orphaned, or poor. The prophet Isaiah declares that we must "learn to do right; seek justice. Defend the oppressed" (1:17) and "maintain justice and do what is right" (56:1). The psalmist affirms that we "uphold the cause of the poor and the oppressed" (82:3), and the apostle James guides us to "look after orphans and widows in their distress" (1:27). Proverbs 3:27 proclaims, "Do not withhold good from those to whom it is due, when it is in your power to act."

In the context of working together to respond to a social struggle, charity as service is a first step if *solving* the social struggle is the end goal, but it can't be the only step. For example, passing out food and blankets to those who are hungry and homeless is only a temporary remedy. Limiting our efforts to such acts of charity can be thought of as serving the struggle rather than serving the solution.

To truly find solutions to social injustice, we need to make a longer-term commitment as the civil right activist Marian Wright Edelman did from a very young age:

> Service was as much a part of my upbringing as eating breakfast and going to school. It isn't something that you do in your spare time. It was clear that it was the very purpose of life. In that context, you're not obligated to win. You're obligated to keep trying, to keep doing the best you can every day.[7]

Moving the principle of service beyond individual acts of charity to a more broad-reaching spirituality might mean helping organize a community coalition, joining a commission dedicated to designing long-term solutions, and organizing and conducting focus groups toward solutions to food insecurity or affordable housing in a community. These can sound like lofty and unattainable goals. However, the more we integrate spiritual principles with far-reaching action, the less lofty and the more attainable these goals will be over time.

Grace

The Presbyterian minister Donald McCullough writes,

---

7. Mariechild, *Open Mind*, 230.

> Grace alone has the power to change people for the better. Only in the capacious freedom of having already been accepted can people own their failure and walk down another path. Grace alone grants the courage to face wrongdoing; grace alone grants the ability to keep things in perspective, to see failure as only one thread in the larger tapestry of life; grace alone grants the strength to rise up with confidence to face a new future.[8]

As such, grace is an essential spiritual principle to understand while working with others to solve a social struggle. However, it can be the most counterintuitive principle to put into practice, whether individually or collectively. Working with others always brings out feelings and opinions about who is worthy and deserving to benefit from our efforts to end a social struggle. But the grace of God—which we are to reflect—is unmerited favor, which means no one is undeserving of it. It is mercy, not merit. Thus, solving any social struggle requires serving everyone: those unemployed or underemployed because of a physical disability, lack of education, or limited skill training; those homeless because of illness, substance use, mental illness, domestic violence, or lack of affordable housing—*everyone*.

During the last couple of decades, I've seen a significant shift among people working together to solve homelessness regarding how and when homeless people obtain temporary and permanent housing. When I first became a case manager in the 1990s, I did what many case managers did, which was to have someone who was homeless earn a shelter bed. Those enrolled in the shelter program had to agree to take any medications that were prescribed for mental illness, to save any earned income in a bank account in their name, and, if they needed support to help with alcohol and drug additions, to attend a twelve-step program. If they did not agree to these three conditions, I told them they were not deserving and ready to enter the shelter program. They could come back when they were. I also told them that if they violated any of the three conditions after entering the shelter program, they would be terminated because they were undeserving of the program.

A low-barrier approach, also known as Housing First, has evolved over the past decade and has been embraced and implemented by stakeholders across the country. Low barrier does not require homeless people to earn their temporary and permanent housing. It does not require sobriety,

---

8. McCullough, *If Grace Is So Amazing*, 169.

medications, and saving earned income. There are no treatment preconditions, behavioral contingencies, or other barriers.

In my work I now promote a low-barrier approach and emphasize that there are not homeless people who are either deserving or undeserving of temporary and permanent housing. When appropriate, I emphasize the grace of God as a divine attribute that is unmerited favor and unearned. It is given to all and everyone.

Piety

Piety is often understood in Christian contexts as an inner and intimate expression of love and loyalty toward God. However, piety as an expression of love and loyalty toward others is not as readily understood. The Scriptures teach us to "love the Lord your God with all your heart and with all your soul and with all your strength and with all your mind, *and your neighbor as yourself*" (Luke 10:27). We love God when we practice compassion and kindness to others. As Father William P. Saunders writes on his popular website Catholic Straight Answers,

> The gift of piety perfects the virtue of justice, enabling the individual to fulfill his [or her] obligations to God and neighbor, and to do so willingly and joyfully. With piety, the person is not only motivated by the requirements of strict justice but also by the loving relationship he [or she] shares with his [or her] neighbor. Simply, a person wants to do what is right in the eyes of God.[9]

Fr. Saunders gives Mother Teresa as an example of someone who embodies the spiritual principle of piety: "Teresa of Kolkata always taught her sisters to treat those they cared for as though they were caring for Jesus Himself, and to do so with a joyful heart and with a smile."[10]

Discernment Guides Our Rule-of-Life Design

Discernment plays a key role throughout the process of developing an integrated rule of life. It is needed to carefully choose spiritual principles that help us walk in the ways of the Lord. As described in the Scriptures,

---

9. Saunders, "What Is the Gift of Piety?"
10. Saunders, "What Is the Gift of Piety?"

discernment is a process of receiving spiritual guidance and understanding. Nouwen describes discernment this way:

> Discernment is a spiritual understanding and an experiential knowledge of how God is active in daily life that is acquired through disciplined spiritual practice. Discernment is faithful living and listening to God's love and direction so that we can fulfill our individual calling and shared mission.[11]

As urban monks, we can use discernment to listen for what causes God is calling us to help solve, what spiritual principles will guide us through the challenges of such work, and what spiritual practices will help sustain us. Discernment can support us as we decide which groups to join to further our goals and how to navigate the complex relationships that come with civic engagement, leadership, and immersion into communities of suffering. Proverbs 16:21 tells us that "the wise in heart are called discerning." Hosea 14:9 explains, "Who is wise? Let them realize these things. Who is discerning? Let them understand. The ways of the LORD are right; the righteous walk in them."

The Scriptures proclaim,

> My son, if you accept my words
>   and store up my commandments within you,
> turning your ear to wisdom
>   and applying your heart to understanding,
> indeed, if you call out for insight
>   and cry aloud for understanding,
> if you look for it as for silver
>   and search for it as for hidden treasure,
> then you will discern the fear of the LORD
>   and find the knowledge of God.
> For the LORD gives wisdom;
>   from his mouth come knowledge and understanding.
> He holds success in store for the upright;
>   he is a shield to those whose walk is blameless,
> for he guards the course of the just
>   and protects the way of faithful ones.
> Then you will understand what is right and just
>   and fair—every good path.
> For wisdom will enter your heart,
>   and knowledge will be pleasant to your soul.

---

11. Nouwen, *Discernment: Reading Signs of Daily Life*, 3.

Spiritual Principles

> Discretion will protect you,
> and understanding will guard you.
> (Prov 2:1–11)

The Scriptures also declare, "For it is God who works in you to will and to act in order to fulfill his good purpose" (Phil 2:13).

The Scriptures tie discernment to spiritual maturity, which is linked to wisdom, knowledge, and understanding. May you discern righteousness, justice, and equity as wisdom enters your heart and knowledge delights your soul as you seek to develop an integrated rule of life.

Reflection Questions

- What spiritual principles will advance your belief that you can help others solve a seemingly intractable social problem?
- What spiritual principles will help you reconcile seemingly irreconcilable conflicting agendas, personalities, and opinions among those people striving to solve a social ill?
- What spiritual principles will help you carry out your words and actions to right a social wrong with others?
- What spiritual principles will help you earn the trust of others while working together to end an entrenched social injustice?

4

Disciplined Spiritual Practices, Part 1
Divine Office of Prayer, Daily Examen, and Lectio Divina

The true intent of a spiritual practice is not about mechanically obeying rules but developing an awareness of the sacred.... Making the sign of the cross is a way to physically express a connection with the suffering of Jesus. Blessing someone when he or she sneezes shows sympathy and concern. These are not just empty rituals. They have the potential to change us inside, to develop our character and make us more aware of our larger responsibility to ourselves, to others, and to God.

—Lewis Richmond

In the early days of my work at the Bad Weather Shelter in Pasadena, when I was serving the overnight shift, I was often overwhelmed by the amount of physical and emotional suffering of the shelter's residents. To shore up my emotional and spiritual strength to serve these people, I began to turn to an increasing number of spiritual practices that had been introduced to me through various books, monasteries, and retreat centers. Compline, examination of consciousness, lectio divina—these and other spiritual practices helped me integrate my winter-shelter experiences into my inner spiritual life and became the foundation of my integrated rule of life, thus initiating my journey as an urban monk.

Spiritual practices help us sustain our commitment to solving social injustices and deepen our relationship to the work, to those we work with and for, and to God. While there are spiritual practices in every faith tradition, I focus primarily on those drawn from my Christian tradition, and I group them into three categories: disciplined, convictional, and impassioned.

Disciplined spiritual practices—such as the Divine Office of Prayer, daily examen, and lectio divina—develop over time through structured teaching within your religious tradition, including school, church, and family.

Convictional spiritual practices arise out of your own experiential learning. They include such practices as incarnational solidarity, which Catholic ethics scholar Kristin Heyer describes as "immers[ing] our bodies and expend[ing] precious energy in practices of presence and service in the real world";[1] and being a wounded healer, a term coined by Carl Jung to describe people who use their own painful experiences to inform their service to others.

Impassioned spiritual practices evolve out of our spiritual passion to move beyond the structure and instruction that shape our disciplined and convictional spiritual practices. These are highly personal practices that energize and revive our spirit, that uplift us and our awareness of God's presence in our life and the lives of those around us. For me, these include praying the Psalms, listening to the blues while praying the Divine Hours of Prayer, and reading the passionate love prayers to Jesus written by Christian mystics.

In this chapter we will focus on three of the more structured disciplined spiritual practices based on reading Scripture and prayer. While some of the spiritual practices are linked to times of the day, they are not prescribed out of a sense of duty or obligation other than a yearning to spend time with God. The structure and instruction that inform these disciplined spiritual practices support an integrated rule of life in that they encourage an ongoing and daily bond with God, which then inspires us to develop a caring relationship with our neighbors.

Divine Office of Prayer

The Divine Office of Prayer involves praying at set times of the day. Historically, up to eight hours of prayer have evolved with each time of prayer

---

1. Heyer, *Kinship across Borders*, 117.

about three hours apart. This disciplined spiritual practice provides an opportunity to have a daylong dialogue with God—not out of a sense of duty or obligation, but out of a sense of commitment and intimacy, which spouses and close friends do on a daily basis. This practice also provides ongoing integrative opportunities to incorporate our daily experiences with others into a time of prayer.

Seven prayer offices have developed over the centuries to help ensure a daylong dialogue with God. As we read in Psalms, "Seven times a day I praise you" (Ps 119:164), with the first office of prayer traditionally beginning in the middle of the night, the second one at 6 a.m., and the rest following every three hours or so.

The Divine Office of Prayer	
Matins/Vigils	3 a.m.
Lauds	6 a.m.
Prime	9 a.m.
Sext	Noon
None	3 p.m.
Vespers	Twilight
Compline	Bedtime

The Daily Office of Prayer has roots in ancient Judaism and was practiced by Jesus. The Gospel of Mark states, "In the morning, while it was still very dark, [Jesus] got up and went out to a deserted place, and there he prayed" (Mark 1:35).

The psalmist did the same:

> I rise before dawn and seek your promises;
> I put my hope in your words.
> My eyes are awake before each watch of the night
> that I may meditate on your promises.
> (Ps 119:147–48)

Early Christians such as Peter, John, and Cornelius continued the Daily Office of Prayer. Acts 3:1 notes, "One day Peter and John were going up to the temple at the time of prayer—at three in the afternoon." Then, "At noon the next day, as they were on their journey and approaching the city, Peter went up on the roof to pray" (Acts 10:9). And later, Cornelius says, "Four days ago, unto this hour, I was praying in my house, at the ninth hour, and behold a man stood before me" (Acts 10:30).

Disciplined Spiritual Practices, Part 1

The Daily Office of Prayer continued throughout the centuries. The Reformation in the sixteenth century gave renewed attention to the Divine Office of Prayer as did the liturgical-renewal movement during the latter part of the twentieth century. Today, the Daily Office of Prayer is practiced in Christian monasteries throughout the world.

The Office Cycle

Four of the prayer offices—Lauds (morning prayer), Sext (noon prayer), Vespers (early evening prayer), and Compline (night prayer)—are more readily practiced in monasteries than the other three. Among these four, two of the offices—Lauds and Compline—are probably practiced more often among laypersons than the other two.

These four offices of prayer provide an opportunity for a continuous cycle of daily prayer that involves consecration, dedication, transition, and contemplation. Below is a brief summary of this continuous cycle of daily prayer:

> ***Morning Hour of Prayer (Lauds):*** The emphasis is on consecration. Let your morning prayer be a time of extraordinary consecration. "I give my life and this day to God for today is a new day" is prayerfully appropriate. "This new day is a gift from God and full of opportunities for service" is also a fitting remembrance.
>
> ***Noonday Hour of Prayer (Sext):*** The emphasis is on dedication. Let your noonday prayer be a time of heightened commitment, for at high noon the sun stands at its apex directly overhead. "I give thanks for the work that I have done so far today" is a helpful reflection, as is "I give thanks for the work that remains today."
>
> ***Twilight Hour of Prayer (Vespers):*** The emphasis is on transition—from our day activities and responsibilities to our night activities and responsibilities. There is a changeover happening around us, particularly if our transitional prayer time occurs around sunset. This time can become very reflective as we look heavenward. It is a time bearing a lot of visual spiritual qualities. The world around us can seem perfectly framed and intensely beautiful even in a dense urban setting. Tall trees are silhouetted against the sky amid a decreasing evening light. Often, as the sun is setting, the clouds begin to glow with colors of water and colors of fire. Buildings may also glow as the sun is reflected

like molten gold on the windows of office buildings, apartments, and houses. Believing that God is saying to you that "you are as intensely beautiful" stimulates a lot of emotions, especially if we allow the words to resonate within ourselves as we go about our evening activities and responsibilities.

Night Hour of Prayer (Compline): The emphasis is on contemplation. *Compline* means "completion" and thus it is this prayer office that completes the circle of the day. Compline is associated with darkness and thus what is hidden and unknown in our lives. There should be an emphasis on discovery that includes finding out how God had been present throughout the day.

The three other prayer offices—Prime (midmorning prayer), None (midafternoon prayer), and Vigils (middle of the night prayer)—enhance a daylong dialogue with God.

Midmorning Hour of Prayer (Prime): One of the historical features of Prime has been the recitation of ancient prayers that have expressed the core of the Christian faith, such as the Athanasian Creed, the Apostles' Creed, or the Nicene Creed. Prime has also been historically characterized by prayers for the work of the day. In the United States, the average workday is often 9 a.m. to 5 p.m. One ancient prayer that can prepare us for the eight-hour workday is the Peace Prayer of St. Francis. The Peace Prayer, as it is known, begins by asking God to make us instruments of peace and ends with recognizing that in daily dying we are born to eternal life.

> Lord, make me an instrument of your peace:
>   where there is hatred, let me sow love;
>   where there is injury, pardon;
>   where there is doubt, faith;
>   where there is despair, hope;
>   where there is darkness, light;
>   where there is sadness, joy.
> O divine Master, grant that I may not so much seek
>   to be consoled as to console,
>   to be understood as to understand,
>   to be loved as to love.
> For it is in giving that we receive,
>   it is in pardoning that we are pardoned,
>   and it is in dying that we are born to eternal life.
> Amen.

Midafternoon Hour of Prayer (None): The two historical characteristics of None are the reading of Psalms and litanies. The readings of Psalms have been historically included in all the hours of prayers, but None consists of mainly Psalms. The Psalms contain prayers that have a full range of human feelings and can be used to express our love and pain as well as our deepest questions or concerns. Litanies include centuries-old forms of public and private prayer that center on invocations and petitions. The invocations generally praise God for the different ways we experience salvation and healing. Petitions generally ask for various graces and blessings.

Middle of the Night Hour of Prayer (Vigils): Vigils (also referred as Night Watch) have historical roots in the predawn vigil of Matins and the dawn vigil of Lauds. Together these two prayer hours bridge the deep darkness of the night with the breaking of light of the new day. It is a time surrounded by darkness and silence that provides occasions for devotional watching or observances. It is also a time of waiting and anticipation.

As the transition from night to day occurs, we can be found waiting for God who "looks down from the heavens" (Ps 33:13) and promises to instruct, teach, and counsel us "with my eye upon you" (Ps 32:8) and my "ears open to [your] cry" (Ps 34:15). At that moment we can know that "when the sun rises, people go out to their work and to their labor until the evening" (Ps 104:22–23). We also know that we are one of them and that we need to weave a sense of love and justice for God and for our neighbors into our daily actions.

A Personal Practice of the Night Watch

The Night Watch is one of the most uniquely powerful spiritual encounters that we can have with God. Jesus began his day very early with prayer. As we read in the Gospel of Mark, "In the morning, while it was still very dark, he got up and went out to a deserted place, and there he prayed" (1:35). The psalmist did the same:

> I rise before dawn and seek your promises;
>   I put my hope in your words.
> My eyes are awake before each watch of the night
>   that I may meditate on your promises.
> (Ps 119:147–48)

I often practice Night Watch by sitting quietly on a small bench facing eastward at Mount Calvary Retreat House in Santa Barbara. I sit quietly, staring at the dark sky, waiting in the predawn hours for the darkness to yield to light. Usually, I hear nothing but the occasional hoot of an owl or the bark of a dog. Sometimes I hear something that sounds like whispering voices, which is probably the wind. I just keep staring into the dark sky, noticing the stars and the moon. Some of the stars seem to disappear and reappear as the night goes on. The North Star stays constant. It makes me dwell on Christ's words: "It is I, Jesus. . . . I am the root and the descendant of David, the bright morning star" (Rev 22:16).

When invisible little birds first begin to chirp, I know that the darkness of the sky is soon going to crack with light. I stare at the dark sky anxiously waiting for the first hint of light.

I like to associate the first hint of light (and subsequent shades and forms of light) with the eye of God piercing the darkness and finding me waiting and ready. As this moment of time approaches, I look toward the heavens and I like to say, "The heavens are telling the glory of God; and the firmament proclaims God's handiwork" (Ps 19:1), and remind myself that "the mighty one, God the Lord, speaks and summons the earth from the rising of the sun" (Ps 50:1), including me.

What fills my heart with anticipation is the divine promise that "light dawns for the righteous, and joy for the upright in heart" (Ps 97:1). The Psalms repeatedly describe the righteous as people whose "delight is in the law of the Lord, and on his law they meditate day and night" (Ps 1:2). I like to hear God saying to me, "I will instruct you and teach you the way you should go; I will counsel you with my eye upon you" (Ps 32:8). This helps me prepare myself for more of God's words.

I find the transition from night to day as a time for waiting and anticipation. Watching the dark gradually turn to light is a natural time for waiting. I like to repeat to myself,

> I wait for the Lord, my soul waits,
>   and in God's word I hope;
> my soul waits for the Lord
>   more than those who watch for the morning.
> (Ps 130:5–6)

Zechariah, the father of John the Baptist, must have been familiar with the above words, as well as the experience of waiting and anticipation as he reflected on the role of his son. He proclaimed,

> By the tender mercy of our God,
>   the dawn from on high will break down upon us,
> to give light to those who sit in darkness
>   and in the shadow of death,
> to guide our feet into the way of peace.
> (Luke 1:78–79)

As the daylight increases so does the shape and color of the eye of God. Shades of dark begin to separate blue from the dark. A long crack of dark blue grows slowly into a longer crack of lighter blue. The first streaks of red appear below the shades of light blue, separating the darker shades of color at the top and the lighter shades at the bottom. Soon a blueish-pink color emerges as the first hint of yellow can be seen. Then the sun appears—an eyeball. I like to say to myself,

> Truly the eye of the LORD is on those who stand in reverence,
>   on those who hope in God's steadfast love. (Ps 33:18)

and hear God saying,

> I will counsel you with my eye upon you. (Ps 32:8)

As the daylight increases so does my need to consecrate this new day to God. The Psalms are full of passages of commitment that consecrate the day through prayer and praise. For example, "But I, O LORD, cry out to you; in the morning my prayer comes before you" (Ps 88:13). I find Psalm 5 to be one of the most intense petitions of prayer in all the Psalms. Several different times within this short passage the psalmist earnestly asks God to listen.

> Give ear to my words, O LORD;
>   give heed to my sighing.
> Listen to the sound of my cry,
>   my King and my God,
>   for to you I pray.
> O LORD, in the morning you hear my voice;
>   in the morning I plead my case to you, and watch.

I experience the time of "watch" as a time of waiting: "For God alone my soul waits in silence; from him comes my salvation" (Ps 62:1). I know that my salvation is secure because "God's steadfast love endures forever" (Ps 136:3). What happens in the heavens each morning makes me want to "declare your steadfast love in the morning" (Ps 92:2) and even "sing aloud of your steadfast love in the morning" (Ps 59:16). Looking up at the early morning sky assures me that God created "the sun to rule over [every] day," which I interpret as a testimony that "his steadfast love [for me] endures forever" (Ps 136:8).

Because of my Christian tradition, it is easy for me to associate God with light during my morning office, particularly because of the way John often applied the symbolism of light to Christ throughout his Gospel and letters (e.g., John 1:4–9; 1 John 1:5–7). For this reason, dawn naturally symbolizes one of the central tenets of my faith—the resurrection of Christ. According to Gospel accounts, Christ's resurrection had occurred by early dawn. His resurrection assures my afterlife with God.

Thus, each morning I associate the crack of dawn with the triumph of life over death. Doing so makes me mindful of my present life on earth. The Psalms make it clear that "the LORD loves justice" (Ps 37:28) and equally clear that I should as well: "The mouths of the righteous utter wisdom and their tongues speak justice," asserts the psalmist. "The law of their God is in their hearts" (Ps 37:30–31).

Bearing this in mind I know that "when the sun rises, people go out to their work and to their labor until the evening" (Ps 104:22–23). I also know that I am one of them, and that a sense of justice needs to be interwoven throughout my daily actions.

The Daily Examen

In 1998 I led a highly transformative initiative to revitalize MacArthur Park, located in the center of Los Angeles. My role was to develop a plan that would create the city's first sidewalk vending program under a recently adopted ordinance by the City Council. It quickly became apparent that the plan would have to address the many social ills experienced by the park and the surrounding neighborhood during the past several decades due to community disinvestment.

After renting a storefront across the street from the park to serve as my office, I was able to get a firsthand look at a deeply wounded area of the city. The sidewalk in front and the thirty-two-acre park across the street were filled daily with illegal document dealers selling *micas* (false documents) to illegal immigrants and others who needed to get work. Drug dealers and drug users openly sold and used. At times, vans along the curbs served as mobile brothels, and people performed sexual acts, either semi-hidden or openly, on the park grounds.

Disciplined Spiritual Practices, Part 1

Few others walked through the park, let alone used it for recreational purposes. To do so meant witnessing drug and sexual activity and to catch glimpses of people off to the side urinating, defecating, and at times masturbating. Those few who did walk through the park were generally street vendors trying to sell food, jewelry, or clothes; preachers yelling into microphones; and volunteers haphazardly passing out food and clothing.

Being engaged in the Bad Weather Shelter and the revitalization of MacArthur Park brought me closer than ever before to many social and physical conditions, such as chronic homelessness, domestic violence, HIV/AIDS, mental illness, physical disability, poverty, substance abuse, and underemployment and unemployment. This fueled the development of my integrated rule of life and my journey as an urban monk. My experiences became increasingly poignant. I can vividly remember spending several months trying to convince a homeless, mentally ill, and substance-abusing man, whom I case-managed for years, to go into detox in preparation for cataract surgery, before he finally did. I distinctly recall community meetings spent trying to persuade elected officials, governmental staff, and appointed commissioners not to further discriminate against homeless people and street vendors who were trying to abide by rules, while others in the meeting expressed prejudice and fear.

During this period, elected officials, governmental staff, businesses, educational institutions, faith-based organizations, neighborhood groups, and nonprofit organizations began to struggle contentiously over issues concerning designing, funding, and locating homeless services and establishing street-vending districts. Even activities such as walking to a store, pumping gas, and using a park or library became emotionally charged for some, as they might encounter someone who was homeless—or seemingly homeless—or a street vendor selling goods without proper equipment and permits.

Getting this close to such woundedness made it difficult to feel or think about anything else. During my years at the Bad Weather Shelter, I often could not sleep when I got home. Because I could not escape the woundedness, I decided to embrace it more and more.

As a teenager, I had heard about St. John of the Cross and one of his writings in particular—the dark night of the soul. (I talk more about the dark night of the soul in a later chapter.) I began to equate my experiences to a dark night of the soul. The more I read about the dark night of the soul, the more I wanted to enter into the experience. According to St. John, it is not the darkness that causes blindness but rather the brilliant light of "divine illumination." I began to associate the rays of divine illumination with the many homeless people that I interacted with. Their woundedness blinded me at first until I decided to delve deeper into the issues that contributed to their pain, such as mental illness and substance abuse. As a result, the rays no longer blinded me but helped me to see and understand the complexity of these issues.

I so wanted to move from the "state of beginners" that St. John describes to the "purified soul." I eagerly sought to climb the "mystic ladder of divine love" that purifies the soul, rung by rung, through prayer, love, and forgiveness. At the same time, I began to fashion my own ladder of service to homeless people based upon my deeper understanding and awareness of compounding factors, such as mental illness.

I could see how the homeless mentally ill were self-medicating with street drugs to deal with their daily debilitating experiences, whether they were taking their prescribed medications or refusing to take them. Most were permanently disabled and unemployable. Their income was generally derived from public assistance and amounted to less than $1,000 a month—not nearly enough for rent, utilities, food, clothing, and other daily necessities. They seemed threatening to property owners and managers and seemed even more threatening to people who, when walking along sidewalks and driving along streets, saw them flailing their arms and murmuring to themselves or shouting to no one in particular. Over time, too many of these people became chronically homeless.

The ladder I fashioned consisted of several rungs that stemmed from my growing compassion and desire to change the trajectory for homeless people, particularly those with mental illnesses. I began to design homeless programs, both residential and nonresidential, that were research-based and proven to be effective. Another rung led to the formation of several coalitions and committees that I initiated, either on my own or with others. Another rung led to grant writing. I began to write public agency grants that helped secure millions of dollars for several counties and cities, and private agency grants that secured thousands of dollars for nonprofit and faith-based organizations. Another rung led to eliminating discriminatory practices in zoning codes that prevented the development of homeless services and led to the adoption of other practices that encouraged the development of professional homeless services. Still another rung led to writing strategies for jurisdictions to end homelessness that were filled with "best practice" recommendations and guidance to implement the recommendations.

I continue to climb this ladder today—the dark night of the soul goes on. In some ways I feel like I am still a beginner, but I know that in other ways my soul has experienced at least some purification and I have climbed high enough to experience divine love. I also continue to use my homeless services ladder to improve the lives of homeless people as well as the life of the larger community.

When I first began to climb this ladder, I turned to the daily examen, a spiritual practice I had heard about as a teenager. Shaped by St. Ignatius of Loyola, the daily examen helps us reflect on God's activity during each day of our lives. We are encouraged to ask God to help us examine ourselves. As part of the examination, we aim to discover how God has been present throughout our day and identify those areas in our lives that need further growth and healing. The assumption is that God spoke and acted within the day, but we may not have heard and recognized it. So, this is an opportunity to take time at the end of day to make sure.

In his Spiritual Exercises, St. Ignatius of Loyola outlines five primary purposes for daily examen:

1. We should thank God for the benefits received that day.
2. We should ask for grace to know and correct our faults.
3. We should pass in review the successive hours of our day, noting what faults we have committed in thought, word, deed, and/or omission.
4. We should ask for God's pardon.
5. We should commit to amendment.

While focusing on these activities, there are several questions that Ignatius encourages us to ask ourselves:

- How has God been present in my day?
- How did God speak to me today?
- How do I feel I was resisting God today?
- How do I feel I was cooperating most fully with God?
- In what ways do I believe God may be calling me to a new awareness?
- What needs healing in my life?

I often add two more questions to this practice: "What did God say to me today that I did not hear?" and "What did God do that I did not see?"

The daily examen is a spiritual practice that helps us reflect, with God's help, on God's activity during our daily life. The Scriptures teach us that God probes the souls of individuals and examines their actions. "I the Lord search the heart and examine the mind, to reward a man according to his conduct, according to what his deeds deserve" (Jer 17:10) and "For a man's ways are in full view of the Lord, and he examines all his paths" (Prov 5:21) are a couple of verses that underline this fact.

The later part of an evening serves as an appropriate time for this type of reflection. As a matter of fact, making a daily examen during Compline can be advantageous. When darkness and night settle in, we may feel a sense of physical rest. Compline, however, may further that sense of relaxation through meditative reflection.

I associate two passages of Scripture closely with daily examen:

> My soul yearns for you in the night,
>   my spirit within me earnestly seeks you. (Isa 26:9)

> My soul is satisfied as with a rich feast,
>   and my mouth praises you with joyful lips
> when I think of you on my bed,
>   and meditate on you in the watches of the night,
> for you have been my help,
>   and in the shadow of your wings I sing for joy.
> My soul clings to you,
>   Your right hand upholds me. (Ps 63:5–8)

The first one emphasizes a strong desire to have God probe our soul and examine the actions of our day. The second passage emphasizes the strong sense of satisfaction while God probes our soul and examines the actions of our day.

Discovering and hearing the voice of God within our own heart, as Ignatius of Loyola reminds us, leads to cooperation with God and healing from God for ourselves and others. We can rest assured that God will speak to us each day. The question is whether we will take the time to make sure that we heard everything that is said to us. Who would not want to hear God saying, "You are precious in my sight, and honored, and I love you," and as a result respond by saying, "I love you too."

Disciplined Spiritual Practices, Part 1

Lectio Divina

Lectio divina is a disciplined spiritual practice that focuses on creating a dialogue with God. The roots of this form of prayer have been traced back to Judaism.[2] Two early church leaders, Origen (185–254) and Ambrose (340–397), are credited with establishing the practice within their cultures. It was Saint Benedict (480–543), however, who promoted and refined its use.[3] Benedict, in his rule for monks,[4] wrote that sacred reading should occur during fixed hours of time (48.1), should be linked with prayer (4.55–56), and should take place during special times of study (ch. 8). In addition, Benedict specified that sacred reading should occur during meals (38.1) and in community gatherings like Vespers and Compline, the final prayer office of the day (ch. 42).

This practice of "divine reading" traditionally involves four steps:

- reading
- meditating
- praying
- contemplating

While *reading* Scripture, you listen to what you are reading and *meditate* on particular sentences, phrases, or words that you feel God is using to communicate with you. As you read, you allow the words "to awaken your heart." The idea is to let the words penetrate your heart, which results in hearing God in your innermost self. The third step, *prayer*, creates an inner dialogue during which you speak from the deepest part of your inner being. The fourth step, *contemplation*, is the process of coming to terms with your inner dialogue, which moves you away from thinking and talking into an area of feeling. Such feelings may be love and compassion toward God and those you want to help; other feelings may be disappointment and outrage toward those who do not want to help the people you want to help.

During my time at the Bad Weather Shelter, lectio divina began to evolve for me as I wanted to take more and more action to help heal the brokenness around me. I read and meditated not only on Scripture passages but on newspaper stories, magazine articles, and books. As I read, I

---

2. Belmonte, "Lectio Divina."
3. Vest, *No Moment Too Small*, 59–62.
4. Benedict, *Rule of St. Benedict*.

hoped that I would discern any specific words or thoughts that I felt were being communicated to me by God. I even reflected on the words I heard from others during coalition or committee meetings to see if God was saying something to me through them.

I soon coupled lectio divina with daily examen. Late at night, when I asked myself, "What did God say to me today that I did not hear?" or "What did God do that I did not see?" I looked for answers by thinking back to what I had read or heard from someone. I would reread a story or reflect on what someone had said during a meeting to discern whether I had missed something that God was trying to communicate to me.

Combining these two practices led me to add two steps to my own lectio divina practice: compassion and action. To enter into union with the divine Word, Christ, is to enter into the hurts and pains of others. We often read that we are to be like Christ. To be like Christ is to embrace the brokenness of our world. This is the Christ who was born in a stable, died between two thieves, and rose from the dead out of a stranger's tomb. This is also the same Christ who "emptied" himself in order to assume our full humanity with all its weaknesses. As noted in the New Testament,

> Though he was in the form of God, [he] did not regard equality with God as something to be exploited, but emptied himself, taking the form of a slave, being born in human likeness. And being found in human form, he humbled himself and became obedient to the point of death—even death on a cross. (Phil 2:6–8)

This "emptying" was for our sake, that he might more fully identify with us so that we could identify with him.

To be Christlike is to be compassionate. There are three linguistic expressions of compassion that underline what it means to be compassionate. The Latin root words literally describe compassion as "suffering together with another." The Greek root words literally describe compassion as "a wrenching of one's guts." The Hebrew root words literally describe compassion as "a powerful emotion of birth that yields personal and societal transformation."

Therefore, being compassionate means to enter the deep wounded heart of the world. This means to identify with the poor, the sick, the imprisoned, the homeless, the dying, the exploited, the oppressed—all whom God identifies with. However, when we open ourselves to the pain of the world, we inevitably open ourselves to our own pain as well. Too often we have experienced brokenness in our own lives and need the transforming embrace of God.

Once we have reached this point, we are at the threshold of action. One course of action could be to begin to avoid our own hurts by avoiding the hurts of others. The other course of action allows God to transform our pain by using us to heal the pain of others.

We begin lectio divina with reading the Word and end with an astonishing intimacy with God. There is nothing left but to move to action—action that will bring healing to others and to ourselves. This means that we need to let others see what we see, hear what we hear, feel what we feel, and be transformed as we are by a loving embrace that causes us to keep coming back to the practice of lectio divina again and again.

For me, such actions led to the creation of another ladder that related to MacArthur Park. One rung was creating a task force of representatives from public and private organizations who were willing to help change the park and surrounding neighborhood. I chaired the monthly meetings, which focused on the next two rungs: "weeding" and "seeding" the area—an idea borrowed from law enforcement. The idea was to weed out the illegal and undesirable activities, such as drug sales, drug use, illegal document sales, and prostitution, then "seed" in desired activities such as concerts, legal street vending, picnics, public art displays, and recreational games. If the seeding doesn't happen, the weeds will grow back. The next rung in this sequence was to acquire the necessary resources to seed desired activities through volunteer efforts and funding from public and private agencies.

Responding to God's Call

Incorporating these practices into your rule of life will help you respond to God's call as expressed through Scripture. As these practices show, responding to Scripture means more than just reading it; rather, reading Scripture creates a dialogue with God—God speaks, and we hear and act. Thus, when God says, "Come now, let's make a covenant, you and I, and let it serve as a witness between us" (Gen 31:44), we can simply respond, "Yes, God, let's make a covenant and let it be a witness between you and me."

When we are daunted by God's invitation to seal a covenant with us, Scripture reassures us of our inherent relationship to God. In Isaiah 44, God declares, "So remember, you are my servant whom I have chosen! And I am the LORD who made you, who formed you in the womb as my servant, whom I have chosen and you shall say, I am the Lord's . . . and write on your hand, 'The Lord's'" (Isa 44:1, 2, 5). At times, I am so personally moved by this verse that I want to literally write on my hand "the Lord's." Another verse exclaims, "I desire to do your will, my God; your law is within my heart" (Ps 40:8).

The source of Jesus's passion was his intense love for humanity, which resulted in his uncompromising commitment to walk a very precise and narrow path to redeem humanity. The Scriptures remind us to imitate his love for humanity because such love should be the source of our own passion and redemption (Phil 2:1–18). They also remind us that the life of Christ provides a pattern for living a passionate life. Through Christ we can experience a spiritual birth that results in the indwelling presence of the Holy Spirit, which leads to a life of continual communion with God. Thus, our living covenant with God is rooted in the passion of Christ.

Perhaps the most powerful words that were given to Christ by the Father and passed on to us concern God and our neighbors. These words are meant to shape our daily thoughts, words, and actions: "Love the Lord your God with all your heart and with all your soul and with all your strength and with all your mind; and 'Love your neighbor as yourself'" (Luke 10:27).

These are the words that should largely shape our integrated rule of life. God clearly wants to write and bind these words into our hearts, souls, and minds as the cornerstone of a divinely initiated living covenant. Developing an integrated rule of life that includes these practices provides the opportunity for God to do so.

Reflection Questions

- How might you integrate ancient and contemporary spiritual practices with your efforts to help right social wrongs?
- Which of the disciplined spiritual practices in this chapter do you feel most drawn to, and why?
- What time of day do you find is most conducive for prayer? How does that align with the Daily Office of Prayer?
- Which spiritual writings and/or writers—ancient or contemporary—have been most influential in your life to date?
- Where might the Daily Office of Prayer, daily examen, and/or lectio divina fit into your efforts to help others solve a social struggle?

5

Disciplined Spiritual Practices, Part 2

Silence, Centering Prayer, and Theological Reflection

> Silence of the heart is necessary so you can hear God everywhere—in the closing of the door, in the person who needs you, in the birds that sing, in the flowers, in the animals.
>
> —Mother Teresa

As urban monks committed to finding solutions to some of society's most challenging problems—and often society's greatest sources of suffering—it can be difficult to quiet our minds enough to connect with God. What we encounter each day is often frustrating, painful, anxiety-inducing, and depressing. Yet, that is often what we need most—to find moments when we truly feel we are in God's presence and can discern what God is asking of us.

In this chapter, I will introduce you to three more disciplined spiritual practices to help you do just that—quiet your mind and spirit and listen for God. Incorporated into your rule of life and practiced regularly, silence, centering prayer, and theological reflection can offer you respite and renewal—sacred space to transform your daily activities and interactions into healing dialogue with God.

Silence

Martin Luther King Jr. said that "our lives begin to end the day we become silent about things that matter." And this is true—as urban monks we are committed to increasing awareness, educating communities, and calling people together to work for solutions to social injustice. But silence can play an important role in connecting us with God and sustaining our spirits and faith in this challenging work.

One of the most basic forms of disciplined spiritual practice is silence. When we think about it in terms of serene solitude with God, silence can be very appealing. But while silent, we need to be ready to hear nonverbal communication from God, which may include feeling the pain of people we have actively or passively interacted with. Silence may become all but silent if we begin to cry out to God in intercessory prayer.

Within the context of religion, silence has long been understood as an important step in spiritual development. Silence has been encouraged in mind and spirit in order for transformative and integral spiritual growth to occur. Centuries ago, Teresa of Avila and St. John of the Cross promoted a prayer of simplicity within the Christian tradition that involved siting in silence while looking upon God with a simple loving gaze. During the past several decades, retreat centers have promoted contemplative prayer as a way of spending time with God in silence. The fruit of a prayer of simplicity and contemplative prayer is experiencing the presence of God in the quiet. As the popular retreat leader Margaret Silf offers,

> Prayer speaks its truth in silence.
> And the silence is understood
> and enfolded back into the silences of space,
> where its energy is not lost,
> but transformed.
> We pray when the words fail
> and only silence suffices.[1]

The Christian Scriptures also encourage silence. "Be still and know that I am God" (Ps 46:10) is a powerful verse when we understand these words as being personally spoken to us by God. Other scriptural calls to quiet include "Listen to me in silence" (Isa 41:1) and "Be still before the Lord" (Ps 37:7). We can respond by saying, "It is good to sit alone in silence

---

1. Silf, *Gift of Prayer*, https://www.spiritualityandpractice.com/explorations/teachers/margaret-silf/quotes.

Disciplined Spiritual Practices, Part 2

when the LORD has imposed it" (Lam 3:27–28), "For God alone my soul waits" (Ps 62:1), or "I wait for the LORD, my soul waits" (Ps 130:5), as a way of heeding God's encouragement to be silent.

Our religious experiences have also understood silence in relationship to sound. One ancient religious saying notes God as telling humans, "You will never be able to hear my words if you cannot hear my silence." Within the context of worship, congregational members are often asked to be silent between prayers and songs to reflect on what was just voiced. In Quakerism, silence is an actual part of worship services and understood as a time to allow the Spirit to speak in the heart and mind of participants. Thus, silence and sound are intertwined.

The folk musician Paul Simon of Simon and Garfunkel wrote "The Sound of Silence" in the aftermath of the assassination of President John F. Kennedy in 1963. His intent was to capture the emotional trauma felt by many Americans through the song's lyrics.

Commemorative silence is another means by which silence is encouraged communally. It is a way of remembering the victims or casualties of a tragic event. In commemorative silence, no one speaks, usually for one or more minutes. One recent example of commemorative silence in a time of turmoil is the moment of silence that is part of an annual memorial concerning the events of 9/11. Each year during these minutes of silence, participants are encouraged to remember and reflect on what happened that day, the people who were directly affected, and our collective response and grief as a nation.

When we practice silence, we may picture ourselves away from the people and places that make up our everyday lives. We may yearn to be high up on a mountain, at the edge of an ocean, or deep within a desert. We may feel it is within these circumstances that we will experience God like never before.

But make no mistake, practicing silence as a way of connecting with God can be challenging. We may experience difficulty keeping silent for any length of time. We may start thinking about the very people and places that we sought to escape. We may start thinking about ourselves—our hurts, insecurities, judgments, desires, responsibilities, obligations. Suddenly, we are unable to remain silent and attentive toward God because our own thoughts become distractions.

It is at this point we realize that silence can be counterproductive and we ask ourselves why. In his book *Contemplative Prayer*, the twentieth-century

Trappist monk and theologian Thomas Merton provided some insight into this dynamic. He noted that we often expect silence to be a medium that results in hearing God speak to us. In other words, we expect God to break our silence with words. However, he believed that silence is the message and not the medium. There is deep communion and communication between us and God through silence, and words will only obscure this union.[2]

If we can obtain lengthy periods of silence, we need to hold ourselves in readiness to hear nonverbal communication from God. In this readiness we will hear God as well as the words of distress, the cries of pain, and the pleas for help that rise from a suffering world—including ourselves. We, in turn, can then present those cries to God in intercessory prayer.

We should remember that the more silent we become, the deeper we are able to go into ourselves. Ordinarily we do not enter such depths because we feel less in control as we journey further inward. Being in such immense silence—hearing God and the hurts and pains of the world—can be frightening.

However, silence can be a very effective tool of integration. It is a spiritual practice that allows us to hold the hurts of others—those we inevitably encounter in our efforts to solve social injustice—and take them to God. As we do so we can deliver our own wounds to God as well. The seventh-century Syrian monk Isaac of Nineveh wrote that

> silence will illuminate you in God . . . and deliver you from phantoms of ignorance. Silence will unite you to God. . . . In the beginning we have to force ourselves to be silent. But then from our very silence is born something that draws us into deeper silence. May God give you an experience of this "something" that is born of silence.[3]

Our integrative experience will only be as deep as our silence.

In the beginning we may have to force ourselves to be silent. Rather than try to avoid our wounds and the wounds of others, we will need to sit in silence with our experiences of alienation, separation, isolation, and loneliness; we will need to hold life's tragedies, such as death, abuse, prejudice, addiction, sickness, and war. As we practice, we will find deep communion and communication with God, and the opportunity for healing.

---

2. Merton, *Contemplative Prayer*.
3. Isaac of Nineveh, *Mystic Treatises*, 299–303.

Disciplined Spiritual Practices, Part 2

Centering Prayer

Centering prayer can provide some structure to our practice of silence and help guide our way to stillness and to God. Centering prayer is a disciplined practice that was largely shaped in the late twentieth century by three Trappist monks—Fathers William Meninger, M. Basil Pennington, and Thomas Keating—at St. Joseph's Abbey in Spencer, Massachusetts. It is a simple method of silent prayer focused on the presence of God. The practice stems from one of the sayings of Christ in the Sermon on the Mount: "But when you pray, go into your room, close the door, and pray to your Father, who is unseen. Then your Father, who sees what is done in secret, will reward you" (Matt 6:6). A more intimate union with God leads to a more powerful experience of God's presence in one's life.

Centering prayer is a popular method of silent contemplative prayer that places a strong emphasis on interior silence and is rooted in the contemplative prayers of the desert fathers and mothers. Guidelines for centering prayer have evolved, and today focus on four primary activities:

1. Sit comfortably with your eyes closed. Relax and quiet yourself.

2. Choose and focus on a sacred word that best supports your desire to be in God's presence—your sacred word could be a name for God such as Mother, Father, Abba, Yahweh, or Adonai; your sacred word could also be a spiritual state or condition such as silence, stillness, peace, calm, or patience.

3. Let your sacred word be gently present as the symbol of your desire to be in God's presence and open to God's presence within you.

4. Whenever you become aware of anything (thoughts, noise, feelings, perceptions, images, etc.), do not engage them, but simply return to your sacred word.

In her book *The Way of Perfection*, the sixteenth-century Carmelite nun and mystic Teresa of Avila describes what she calls the "prayer of quiet":

> I would warmly recommend to all, never to finish prayer without remaining some little time afterward in a respectful silence. As soon as the soul by faith places itself in the presence of God, and becomes contemplated before our Lord, let it remain thus for a little time in respectful silence.
>
> In forming this act of faith, (if) it feels some little pleasing sense of the Divine presence, let it remain there without being

troubled for a period, and proceed no farther, but carefully cherish this sensation while it continues. When it abates, it may excite the will by some tender affection; and if, by the first moving thereof, it finds itself reinstated in sweet peace, let it there remain.[4]

For Teresa, the experience is like sitting very close to someone you love deeply and not needing words to express the deeper level of the relationship. It's pure communion and not conversation. You can remain in silence and even close your eyes and sense the depth of the relationship.

Centering prayer is not an active mode of prayer. It is a receptive mode of prayer. It prepares us to experience God as close as our consciousness, thoughts, breathing, and feelings time and time again. The purpose is not to seek an altered state of consciousness but rather to experience the closeness of our relationship with God, which we may not be fully aware of until we take time to realize and recognize it. As Thomas Keating explains,

> Don't judge centering prayer on the basis of how many thoughts come or how much peace you enjoy. The only way to judge this prayer is by its long-range fruits: whether in daily life you enjoy greater peace, humility and charity. Having come to deep interior silence, you begin to relate to others beyond the superficial aspects of social status, race, nationality, religion, and personal characteristics.[5]

In centering prayer, in listening to the silence, we learn that we cannot stop thoughts or feelings from coming up. We also learn not to be surprised by our thoughts or intense feelings. We discover that God wants to communicate all sorts of things to us that we otherwise would not know, especially about civic engagement and solutions to social struggles. Thus, centering prayer cultivates a relationship with God that is both deeply rewarding and personally challenging.

Theological Reflection

Theological reflection was also introduced during the late twentieth century as a practice of reflecting on life events in relation to one's faith. It has evolved into a disciplined practice that seeks meaning and illumination of a particular life situation through the joined sources of Scripture and faith.

---

4. Teresa of Avila, *Way of Perfection*, 153–54.
5. Iachetta, *Daily Reader for Contemplative Living*, 18.

Disciplined Spiritual Practices, Part 2

Thus, when we practice theological reflection, we aim to confirm, challenge, clarify, and expand how we understand life's experiences. Meaningful theological reflection involves hearing something new or unexpected, which may move our faith into action.

In theological reflection we form an ongoing or concluding thought or opinion about an encounter between ourselves and another person(s) or place(s) based on the belief that God is incarnational—that is, present in the world today; providential—God cares about the world today; and revelational—God communicates with the world today. We also draw upon our Christian heritage—its denominational teachings, sermons, books, Sunday School lessons, interpretation of Scripture, and so on—that has shaped our views, values, convictions, and beliefs about the many different people and places we encounter in our daily lives.

As we practice theological reflection, we look deeply at a specific event or encounter through the lens of Christian faith: What really happened? Who was there? How did we react? How do we wish we responded? Where was God in the experience? As a result of this work, we may take a different course of action to deal with an ongoing encounter or ready ourselves for a similar encounter in the future. We may feel challenged to think and act differently—perhaps more in line with our spiritual principles. We may begin to question or discard previously held beliefs. Most importantly, the process of theological reflection can help us overcome our tendency to avoid a challenging social struggle.

The process consists of three primary action steps:

1. Attending
2. Asserting
3. Deciding

Attending brings three primary sources of experience—personal, religious, and cultural—into an inner dialogue with ourselves or an outer dialogue with others, noting the congruences and incongruences between and among these experiences. Congruences are not likely to be as challenging as incongruences. When we look deeper into our experiences, we may be challenged by the values, mores, convictions, and struggles of others that we may not have heard before. For example, we may have never understood the impact of trauma on someone who lost their housing because of a traumatic experience such as domestic violence, human trafficking, and/or sexual assault. It may be difficult for us to understand why a woman would *choose* to be homeless even though she is clearly traumatized by the experience of homelessness. But then we learn that she made that choice because her only other option was to return to her abuser, who lives in her home—it's her conviction to never return to conditions of abuse. We need to be able to hear something new or unexpected if we are to engage in meaningful theological reflection.

Asserting follows attending because it helps us embrace the congruences and incongruences of our daily experiences. We may state with confidence our opinions, convictions, or principles that seemingly align with God's guidance. For example, we may never have believed that someone would choose to be homeless or why a homeless person would reject our efforts to restore their living situation. But now that we are familiar with the circumstances and convictions of the woman who chooses homelessness rather than returning to an abusive home, we can bring this understanding into our advocacy for change. Assertion is also needed to tolerate ambiguity during theological reflection. As we gain new insights; something we have held to be true for a long time may no longer hold true. This may result in asserting the new truth, which can be a liberating process but also a painful one. As Hebrews 4:12–13 puts it,

> The word of God is living and active. Sharper than any double-edged sword, it penetrates even to dividing soul and spirit, joints and marrow; it judges the thoughts and attitudes of the heart. Nothing in all creation is hidden from God's sight. Everything is uncovered and laid bare before the eyes of him to whom we must give account.

The action steps of attending and asserting slow down our usual processes of interpreting our exchanges with others. This takes courage because it makes us vulnerable in a couple ways: we may reexperience such feelings as anger, fear, humility, or grief, and we may open ourselves to reinterpret our most dearly held opinions, convictions, or principles. In the case of working with homeless people, having this deeper understanding of trauma and the fear of retraumatization can be transformative in how we approach championing efforts to find solutions. The actions we take may also involve revisiting and revising our integrated rule of life with this newfound understanding.

However, the goal of theological reflection is *deciding*, which marks the moment in the practice of theological reflection when we choose to respond to the call of integration. It is the point at which we move from

Disciplined Spiritual Practices, Part 2

faith into action, convinced of God's incarnational, providential, and revelational involvement in our everyday public and private worlds.

These three disciplined practices can help an urban monk craft their integrated rule of life as they discern which social struggle they feel called to and which spiritual practices have the greatest influence in their quest to consistently serve others through their highest selves. These practices can also help strengthen the urban monk as they willingly encounter and engage the most vulnerable people and places on the front lines of working for a solution to their social struggle.

Reflection Questions

- What are the spiritual principles that have guided you throughout your life and how might you transform them into spiritual practices to help restore and renew your spirit as you work with others to help solve social struggles?
- What do you find are the most challenging aspects of practicing silence?
- What are a few sacred words that you might like to use as focal points in centering prayer to realize God's presence?
- What is an especially challenging aspect of your current work to find solutions to your social struggle that may benefit from processing through theological reflection?

6

Convictional Spiritual Practices

> We have been given the gift of life in this perplexing world to become who we ultimately are: creatures of boundless love, caring compassion, and wisdom. Existence is a summons to the eternal journey of the sage—the sage we all are, if only we could see.
>
> —Wayne Teasdale

MERRIAM-WEBSTER DEFINES CONVICTION AS "the act or process of finding a person guilty of a crime especially in a court of law." In Christianity, it can mean to convince of sin; to prove or determine to be guilty, as by the conscience. In this understanding, conviction is produced by the Holy Spirit, the gospel, conscience, and the Law, and brings with it an awareness of sin that ideally results in repentance. What *I* mean by *conviction* reflects another meaning: *a strongly held belief.* Therefore, convictional spiritual practices express firmly held attitudes or beliefs that compel us to action and are energized by glimpses of solutions for seemingly intractable social ills and issues. These practices also cultivate spiritual development that moves us along a path filled with opportunities to integrate interactions between God, others, and ourselves.

Convictional spiritual practices express an attitude rooted in the idea that our lives and all that we have should be shared with others—whether we know them or not. Integrating our everyday interactions with the intention of reconciliation has the potential for healing, long overdue.

As part of an integrated rule of life, convictional spiritual practices can help prepare us and ultimately move us into action, which is crucial for civic engagement.

Incarnational Solidarity

As part of our rule of life, the practice of incarnational solidarity can help sustain our understanding of the big picture—we are all one. The underlying consideration concerning incarnational solidarity is threefold:

1. If all is not well with others, all is not well with you.
2. If all is not well with you, then all is not well with others.
3. If all is not well with you and others, then all is not well with God.

During a speech delivered at the National Cathedral in Washington, DC, on March 31, 1968, Martin Luther King Jr. stated,

> In a real sense all life is interrelated. All persons are caught in an inescapable network of mutuality, tied in a single garment of destiny. Whatever affects one directly affects all indirectly. I can never be what I ought to be until you are what you ought to be. And you can never be what you ought to be until I am what I ought to be. This is the interrelated structure of reality.[1]

Within this framework, solidarity provides deep-rooted feelings of community and union. Adding the Christian concept of incarnation within this context means that we recognize God as part of the inescapable network of mutuality—we are woven together into a single garment of destiny.

An inescapable network of mutuality can be ignored but not eliminated. All of us share the physical and emotional fabric that make up our everyday lives. The physical fabric of our private lives is primarily our home. The physical fabric that makes up our public lives includes streets, sidewalks, buildings, and open spaces that many of us use every day. Privately, we may live with family and friends and share meals, watch movies, play games, and so forth. Publicly we drive alongside one another, walk past one another, work and shop together, and share parks, beaches, plazas, and more for recreation and leisure. These private and public experiences bring

---

1. In Washington, ed., *I Have a Dream*, 85.

us into contact with one another. As a result, we are often confronted with one another's living experiences. Some experiences are easy to witness or embrace—getting married, having a baby, working a great job, or going on a vacation, for example. Other experiences are not so easy to embrace—alienation, loneliness, prejudice, discrimination, addiction, sickness, death, and so on.

Solidarity is rooted in mutual giving and receiving. When we enter into the experience of another person or group of people as an act of solidarity, whether the experience is one of joy or pain, it is meant to be an ongoing process, not a one-time occurrence. Thus, we become "solid" or whole with another person.

The Essence of Incarnation

The core of the Christian doctrine of incarnation is the union of God and humanity in the person of Jesus Christ. The starting place within the New Testament is the annunciation, recorded in Luke: the revelation to Mary by the angel Gabriel that she will conceive a child to be born the Son of God, which will fulfill the prophecy of Isaiah that a virgin (or maiden) would bear a son who would be called Immanuel ("God with us"):

> The angel said to her, "Do not be afraid, Mary, you have found favor with God. You will be with child and give birth to a son, and you are to give him the name Jesus. He will be great and will be called the Son of the Most High. . . . The Holy Spirit will come upon you, and the power of the Most High will overshadow you." And Mary responds by saying "I am the Lord's servant" and "May it be to me as you have said." (Luke 1:35–38)

This encounter between the angel and Mary is understood within Christianity as the moment when the Holy Spirit descended and came to dwell among women and men. Later Christian writings and traditions have come to understand Mary as the archetype of all humanity. She sees herself as the Lord's servant and submits to the indwelling of God through the Holy Spirit.

For centuries, contemplatives have looked upon the attitude and words of Mary as multivalent. On the one hand, they relate to the salvific mystery that Jesus initiated before his ascension to heaven (Matt 28:19). On the other hand, they relate to a continuing occurrence that has taken place within the bodies and hearts of Christian disciples since then. Like Mary, disciples of Christ are finite earthen vessels into which infinite divine life is poured. Thus, the one who created you is created in you.

The essence of incarnation is embedded in the indwelling of God through the Holy Spirit. Prior to his resurrection, Christ promises his disciples the Holy Spirit. In chapter 14 of the Gospel of John, Jesus tells his disciples that he "will ask the Father, and he will give you another Counselor to be with you forever—the Spirit of truth. The world cannot accept him because it neither sees him nor knows him. But you know him, for he lives with you and will be in you" (John 14:16–17). Later in the chapter, Jesus also says, "The Counselor, the Holy Spirit, whom the Father will send in my name, will teach you all things and will remind you of everything I have said to you" (John 14:26).

The fulfillment of Christ's promises is narrated in the book of Acts. In the first chapter, Jesus tells his disciples, "Do not leave Jerusalem, but wait for the gift my Father promised, which you have heard me speak about. For John baptized with water, but in a few days you will be baptized with the Holy Spirit" (Acts 1:4–5). The second chapter records the fulfillment of the promise:

> When the day of Pentecost came, they were all together in one place. Suddenly a sound like the blowing of a violent wind came from heaven and filled the whole house where they were sitting. They saw what seemed to be tongues of fire that separated and came to rest on each of them. All of them were filled with the Holy Spirit. (Acts 2:1–4)

It's Contact, Not Concept

Incarnational solidarity is largely learned through contact rather than through concept. Conceptually, solidarity is steeped in the ideals of community and union as well as in the indwelling of God through the Holy Spirit Christ promised to his disciples. However, the essence of incarnational solidarity is learned through contact with those who make up our private and public lives. Through contact we learn about the many experiences that our family members, friends, coworkers, and strangers have each day. These experiences can be difficult—a family member's sickness, a friend's loss of a loved one, a coworker's substance abuse problem, or a stranger's state of homelessness.

Incarnational solidarity then takes us beyond learning about people's lives to walking with them and offering support as they struggle through it. As Martin Luther King Jr. emphasized, "Whatever affects one directly affects all indirectly." When we practice incarnational solidarity as part of our rule of life, the inadequacies, hurts, and injustices that we all experience become the means by which we become who we truly are in the eyes of God as we help others realize their own true potential. In Christianity, Jesus is our model: the hurts, suffering, and death of Jesus reveal the purpose of his existence, which is resurrection, eternal life, and permanent healing.

As urban monks and disciples of Christ, we can stand in incarnational solidarity with others—with Christ standing in our midst. Together we can mourn someone's death, heal from a divorce, overcome the loss of a job, gain sobriety, or work to overcome a physical or mental disability. Incarnational solidarity is embedded in acts of mutual giving and receiving that lead to healing and allow us and others to "be what we ought to be."

An urban monk might live this out by accompanying a person with substance abuse problems as they seek resources and treatment, staying with them and lending support as they go through what can the agonizing experience of detoxification, showing up for them when they need a shoulder to lean on as they journey toward sobriety, accepting relapse as part of the recovery process, and assuring them of your unconditional friendship.

Incarnational solidarity also goes beyond one-to-one experience. It is equally important to stand in incarnational solidarity with others. These groups may be, geographically speaking, as small as a portion of a neighborhood or as large as a district, city, county, or country.

While we are practicing incarnational solidarity, we may find ourselves asking questions: How can I be rich if my neighbor is poor? How can I experience equality if residents in my city are experiencing inequality? How can I not be hungry or be in good health if people in another region or country are hungry or in poor health? Raising these questions often puts us into a different type of relationship with others. It is not a direct one-to-one relationship but a one-to-many. It is a relationship that may or may not include direct contact initially but is marked with empathy. Our empathy can result in feeling the intensity of others' woundedness and may even lead to find ways to establish direct contact—we may be called into action by our empathy. Whether we are in relationship with one individual or many, the underlying consideration of incarnational solidarity is our interrelatedness within a common human reality.

The Wounded Healer

Henri Nouwen made *wounded healer* synonymous with *minister*. Nouwen describes wounded healers as individuals who "must look after [their] own wounds but at the same time be prepared to heal the wounds of others."[2] The minister is one who wants to serve others. However, the minister is a wounded person. The same is true of the urban monk, and formally recognizing within our rule of life that our work is that of a wounded healer can help fortify us on the formidable journey to finding solutions to social injustices.

Nobody escapes being wounded. We are all wounded people—physically, emotionally, mentally, or spiritually. Nouwen specifically raises the question: What are our wounds? He notes that words such as *alienation, separation, isolation,* and *loneliness* express our wounded condition. In *Being a Wounded Healer: How to Heal Ourselves While We Are Healing Others*, the author Douglas C. Smith answers the same question by describing our woundedness in terms of life's tragedies, including divorce, death, abuse, addiction, sickness, and mental illness.

Experiences such as alienation, separation, isolation, and loneliness cause wounds but also serve as expressions of our woundedness. We often experience these wounding incidents through other people. Others may speak or act in ways that leave us feeling dissociated, dejected, companionless, misunderstood, depressed, abused, violated, or hurt. We may feel embarrassed, insecure, rejected, or inferior. Our wounds may have been inflicted upon us unintentionally or intentionally.

Life's tragedies can be profoundly wounding. Family members and friends can be wrenched from us through divorce and death. Divorce is too often marked by abuse, which can be both verbally and physically scarring to spouses and children. A sudden death of a loved one can leave us without words to express our unexpected heartbreak, while a prolonged death can leave us devastated and pained, even when the heartbreak is expected. Chronic and degenerative diseases, war wounds, paralysis, rape, and other traumatic experiences can be equally cruel and inflict deep wounds into our souls and the souls of others. We carry all our wounds into our work as urban monks.

Wounded healers not only tend to their own wounds and the wounds of family members and friends but also to those of strangers. They prepare

---

2. Nouwen, *Wounded Healer*, 82.

for this service by realizing two primary insights about their own wounds: they are not a source of shame, and can be a source of healing.

We often want to hide our wounds. Our wounds may cause us to feel depressed or insecure, or to fear rejection. We may be unsure about what other people's reaction will be once they know about our woundedness.

We become wounded healers when we cope effectively with our own feelings of alienation, separation, isolation, and loneliness, and with the aftermath of life's tragedies. The ability to heal stems from a deep understanding of one's own pain, which provides the opportunity to convert weaknesses into strengths and to then offer one's strength as a source of healing for others.

Nouwen notes that a wounded healer's primary task is not to take away the pain but to deepen it to a level where it can be shared. This deepening process begins a shared journey to healing and transformation. We feel wounded when others are wounded: I feel with, and for, others and therefore our shared journey prevents me from distancing myself from others. As Nouwen explains, "A Christian community is therefore a healing community not because wounds are cured and pains are alleviated but because wounds and pains become openings or occasions for a new vision."[3]

The Spiritual Canticle by St. John of the Cross captures the power of one's healing presence toward another's woundedness. It is a loving exchange, filled with the images found in the Song of Songs, between Christ the Bridegroom and a bride, who is us. Such images are used to express the pains, longings, and desires between the two.

In the Spiritual Canticle, the Bridegroom compares himself to a stag. It is characteristic of the stag to climb to high places, and if wounded, race in search of refreshment and cool waters. If he hears the cry of his mate and senses that she is wounded, he "immediately runs to her to comfort and caress her." Among lovers, the wound of one is a wound for both, and the two have but one feeling.

As wounded healers, we wait for and listen to the other's thoughts and feelings. We pause in our caregiving to feel the intensity of the other's woundedness. When we do so, we experience compassion, which begins the mutual process of healing.

---

3. Nouwen, *Wounded Healer*, 94.

Integration of Material and Spiritual Poverty

In their discernment of a social injustice on which to focus, many urban monks will identify some kind of material poverty they wish to bring an end to. But in drafting a rule of life and setting goals for our efforts, we need to abandon any idea of a dichotomy between material and spiritual poverty if we truly want to achieve justice and healing.

Material poverty is often defined in very basic terms: the lack of food, clothing, and shelter. But there are also social circumstances that contribute to material poverty: the lack of education, employment, health care, and political power. An inability to sufficiently access these resources often results in unequal social status, inequitable social relationships, social exclusion and/or expulsion, and a diminished capacity to participate in processes that may change social and economic conditions.

In essence, we are all materially impoverished. As previously noted, the Scriptures make it clear that "the earth is the Lord's and all that is in it, the world, and those who live in it" (Ps 24:1). Before God, each one of us is poor, whether or not we experience economic circumstances that make us materially poor.

Spiritual poverty is a result of a broken relationship with God, and therefore can be more challenging to identify. Some common signs of spiritual impoverishment include feelings of unworthiness, hopelessness, and shame. A person who is spiritually poor feels unloved, rejected, and enveloped in a sense of lack, maybe even feeling deserving of their conditions. Acknowledging the reality and destructiveness of spiritual poverty in our rule of life and identifying our own broken relationships with God can help us more easily identify it and address it in others. We are all broken and poor before God and one another.

Both types of impoverishments jeopardize a person's physical and mental health as well as the community as a whole. When these experiences are a reality for others, they are a reality for us; when they are a reality for us, they are a reality for others. This is the inescapable network of economic and social mutuality that should not be ignored and must be eliminated.

All of us share the material and spiritual fabric that make up our everyday lives. The way out of material and spiritual poverty for us and others needs to include prayer. Our prayers should stem from how God sees us—that is, as poor and rich at the same time. We are poor in that the earth and all that it contains is God's, not ours. The earth contains resources that are God's, and we must help ensure these resources are shared by all.

Prayer alone is not enough. Ministry is needed, and our rule of life helps to shape that sacred service. Our ministry should help ensure that resources are shared. This includes ensuring adequate food, clothing, and shelter, but also actively building relationships with the impoverished, providing spiritual direction, and advocating for social and political capital. Through these efforts we can break a cycle of dependence that keeps others and ourselves from fully healing from this brokenness.

Monastic Cell

The word *cell* has a long monastic tradition referring originally to the monk's cave or room. Monastic writings often note that the monk who lives in a cell lives in a sacred place. The English word for cell comes from the Latin word *cella*, which means "small chamber" (akin to the Greek word *naos*, meaning "inner chamber of a temple").

Throughout history, the word *cell* has been used with religious connotations to signify a physical space designated for spiritual use. In ancient Egypt, the cell was a completely walled space inside the inner sanctum of a temple. It existed in complete darkness, symbolizing the state of the universe before the act of creation, with emphasis placed on the hidden and unknown.

In ancient Greek and Roman temples, the cell was a room at the center of the building, usually containing a cult image or statue and/or a table or pedestal to receive votive offerings. In early Christian and Byzantine architecture, the cell was an area at the center of the church reserved for performing the liturgy as a collective public experience for congregants.

Over the centuries, what defined the cell broadened beyond a private, physical space to include the private experience of having a spiritual relationship with God. Early monastic writings are filled with metaphors that emphasize the monastic cell as a place for the monk to withdraw from the world and cultivate their spiritual life in solitude and silence. After the twelfth century, however, monastic writings began to contain metaphors describing the monastic cell as not only a place withdrawn from the world, but also as a place within the world where a monastic could still experience solitude and silence amid outdoor beauty.

Convictional Spiritual Practices

The cell was no longer limited to the monk's physical room but became any place—a garden, for example—that offers solitude and silence in which someone could cultivate a deeper relationship with God. The cell can also be the quiet of our inner selves:

> Said the teacher, "Go sit within your cell
> and your cell will teach you wisdom."
> The disciple said, "But I have no cell. I am no monk."
> The teacher said, "Of course you have a cell. Look within."[4]

The soul is a place where we can find solitude and silence amid everyday life. It is a place where we can connect with God at any moment and cultivate an ongoing interior relationship with God. Because it doesn't require an arduous journey or material resources to get there, it is a sacred healing destination readily available to anyone and everyone:

> Is the path to enlightenment difficult or easy?
> It is neither.
> Why not?
> Because it is not there.
> Then how does one travel to the goal?
> One does not. This is a journey without distance.
> Stop traveling and you will arrive.[5]

Readily available doesn't necessarily mean it's easy to get there. Our fast-paced modern world makes it ever more challenging to prioritize time and make space for the silence and solitude needed to connect with our soul and our relationship with God:

> The teacher said
> It is easier to travel than to stop.
> The disciples demanded to know why.
> The teacher said
> Because as long as you travel to a goal,
> you can hold on to a dream.
> When you stop, you face reality.[6]

It may feel counterintuitive to enter your inner cell, or soul, in the midst of your everyday urban experiences. Even the word *urban* conjures images of people with complex problems living in crowded and congested

---

4. De Mello, *One Minute Wisdom*, 14.
5. De Mello, *One Minute Wisdom*, 50.
6. De Mello, *One Minute Wisdom*, 51.

areas—think teeming sidewalks, crawling traffic, busy offices, and noisy stores, but also homeless encampments, drug dens, shelters at capacity, and seemingly endless people in need.

We might use our rule of life to remind us that we can access our inner cell at any time. Connecting with our soul while walking along a crowded street and passing by someone in need, or while waiting for a traffic light to change and observing panhandlers and peddlers, provides us with opportunities to further our process of integration. Finding God amid the people that make up our everyday urban life reminds us that our relationship with God is always lived out in the context of relating with one another and the whole created order.

Accessing our soul is not an escape from the world, but rather the place and time we continually discover, affirm, empower, and transform our loving service to God and others.

Reflection Questions

- Describe some experiences you've had where you've served as a wounded healer. What qualities helped shape that service?
- Describe an experience you've had where you've been served by a wounded healer. What were their qualities?
- Where are some special places in your life that you find especially conducive to contemplation—places that might serve as your "monastic cell"?
- In your efforts to find solutions to your social struggle, how does material poverty and spiritual poverty manifest among those you serve and those you serve with?
- How might convictional spiritual practices, as part of your integrated rule of life, help you in finding solutions to your social struggle?

7

Impassioned Spiritual Practices

The word of God is living and active. Sharper than any double-edged sword, it pierces even to dividing soul and spirit, joints and marrow. It discerns the thoughts and intentions of the soul.

—Hebrews 4:12

Over a decade ago, while practicing lectio divina I came across these lines in Psalm 31:

> I am the scorn of all my adversaries,
>   a horror to my neighbors,
> an object of dread to my acquaintances,
>   those who see me in the street flee from me.
> I have passed out of mind like one who is dead;
>   I have become like a broken vessel.
> (vv. 11–12)

At the time, I was a social worker providing case management services to people experiencing homelessness, including veterans who had served during the Vietnam War. I reread verses 11 and 12 and meditated on them several times over the next few weeks. I could not help but think of the veterans I was working with and the feelings they had shared with me about their experiences of homelessness.

They told me about the "thousand-yard stare"—the unfocused gaze of a battle-weary soldier who wanted distance from the unpleasant things he saw too often while serving in Vietnam. They described how they were on the receiving end of that stare now that they were homeless and walking the streets. People would look down in front of them, to the side of them, or right through them as though they were not there.

They knew people did not want to be reminded about homelessness, but they also knew that some people struggled with how to respond to them. The trauma they had witnessed as active soldiers abroad was compounded by the rejection they felt as inactive homeless veterans at home. As I struggled to keep focused on them and their social service needs, their pain became my pain. It was in this way that my disciplined practice of lectio divina became an impassioned practice.

Being impassioned can be viewed as suspect or unacceptable, especially by others. It can be viewed as feelings of annoyance, displeasure, and disappointment instead of inspiration and enthusiasm.

There are times, however, when we tap into our passion and move beyond a learned experience to one that is energizing and reviving. Not only do we find what evolves out of our passion as pleasing and fulfilling, but others reinforce these rewarding passionate experiences when they come to understand what we have accomplished. They witness how an impassioned person who is deeply committed to bringing healing to a social pain can cultivate emotions in others that inspires them to take action, too.

Impassioned spiritual practices are disciplined spiritual practices that are emotionally resonant and highly personalized when they are practiced in reflection of what you're deeply passionate about. For urban monks, this is often the social injustice to which they've dedicated their lives and work to solving—the cause itself, the people they serve, and the people they work with. As such, as part of an integrated rule of life, these impassioned practices can continuously nourish and renew the urban monk's spirit and commitment to their chosen social struggle.

The impassioned practices I describe below are disciplined practices that I integrated into my life, but they became seemingly undisciplined after I tapped into my passion and moved beyond the conventional structure and instruction shaping each discipline. These examples disclose how an intense passion added more fuel to my desire to solve social struggles. My impassioned spiritual practices stem from the various ways prayer and reading of Scripture are practiced today, which evolved out of the way others began praying decades or even centuries ago. But any spiritual practice can become impassioned when infused with the fire to enact lasting change and transformative healing for ourselves and others.

Praying the Psalms

Authentic prayer emerges when we dare to express our pain and raise before God our deepest questions and concerns, as we see on the Psalms:

> Out of the depths I cry to you, O Lord.
> Lord, hear my voice. (Ps 130:1)

> O Lord, God of my salvation,
>   when, at night, I cry out in your presence,
> let my prayer come before you;
>   incline your ear to my cry,
> For my soul is full of troubles. (Ps 88:1–3a)

Prayer remains a somewhat shallow affair if we leave out the full range of our feelings.

> My throat thirsts for you,
>   My body aches for you. (Ps 63:1b)

> God heals the brokenhearted
>   and binds up their wounds. (Ps 147:3)

> The Lord is near to the brokenhearted,
>   and saves the crushed in spirit. (Ps 34:18)

> For the needy shall not always be forgotten,
>   nor the hope of the poor perish forever. (Ps 9:18)

Tapping into one's passion while reading and praying the Psalms can easily move one beyond a disciplined practice of reading and praying Scripture to an impassioned practice of embodying these texts, for the Psalms are prayers containing the full range of human emotions. Several of the Psalms are written in couplets, which are paired lines that bear close relation to each other, where the second part of the couplet frequently intensifies or heightens the meaning of the first part. As urban monks, there are times when what we experience on a given day may best be dealt with by daring to express our deepest questions and concerns, or perhaps our fears or pains, to God. When we use the Psalms to convey these emotions and feelings of vulnerability, the practice becomes impassioned.

Divine Office of Prayer and the Blues

Over the years, the Divine Office of Prayer evolved for me into hours for the blues because I choose to spend significant time during these hours reflecting on my personal plights and those within the communities in which I live, work, worship, socialize, and serve. I first learned to practice the Divine Office of Prayer collectively in Christian monasteries during day visits and retreats. As described earlier, monasteries have set hours of divine prayer that follow the traditional times of prayer or canonical hours established over the centuries. (For a reminder of the specific times, please see chapter 4.)

I began to practice the Divine Office of Prayer on my own, particularly at home. The hour of prayer that I kept most often was around midnight since I am a night owl who would rather stay up late than get up early in the morning. During my "Divine Hour of the Midnight Blues," I often found myself spending long periods of reflection that centered on personal issues with relationships, career development, and social issues such as poverty and unemployment. Such times were constantly filled with angst, despair, grievances, helplessness, hurt, and other similar feelings.

The blues are a genre of music filled with expressive lyrics and emotions that over the decades permeated the bars and clubs of cities like Chicago, where I grew up. Not only did the lyrics of these songs strike a spiritual chord but the titles did as well: "Midnight Blues," "Three O' Clock Blues," "Six O' Clock Blues"—each comparable to a time for the Divine Office of Prayer.

The hours for the blues have a history that goes back a couple of hundred years. Originating among African Americans living in the US southern states, the blues have been described as the essence of the African American laborer, whose spirit is wed to these songs, reflecting their inner soul to all who will listen. The lyrics are often filled with chants of sorrow, lost love, the harsh realities of life, yearnings to be free from life's troubles, and the ongoing journey of a lost soul longing for redemption. I heard such lyrics throughout the years in the songs sung by some of the great blues musicians like B. B. King, Muddy Waters, KoKo Taylor, and Dinah Washington.

I made parallels between the emotional expressions found within the Scriptures, which have been devoutly dedicated for use for the Divine Office of Prayer, and the emotional expressions found within blues lyrics—feelings of hurt, wounding, wanting, grievance, and injustice, among others. Similar emotions can also be found in many verses of the book of

Psalms, the one book of the Bible that has been used more often than any other during the Divine Office of Prayer.

Another parallel that I made is to the times of the day that have been faithfully marked and encouraged by these distinct but spiritually related practices. My own cries for justice occurred more and more often during my Divine Hour of the Midnight Blues, and as my personal life concerning relationships, educational pursuits, and career became more and more complex. Equally complex, if not more so, were my increasing experiences of community involvement with social issues, which included support for affordable housing, ending homelessness, small business and job development, substance abuse treatment, mental health care, and ending discriminatory practices such as redlining, steering, and implementation of prejudicial zoning ordinances that resulted in civil rights violations. As a result, these hours of prayer evolved into times for reflection and emotional prayer.

Faithfulness, comfort, and healing are also the focus of many of the Psalms, which helped strengthen me throughout these troubling and challenging experiences. I found myself willing to embrace bouts with my own blues during my hours of prayer and finding spiritual nourishment and renewal. I am convinced that engaging the blues, as both feelings and lyrics, during a personal or collective Divine Office of Prayer as part of your integrated rule of life will help you reach new depths in your relationship with God and generate more fuel and fire for personal and societal transformation.

Passionate Love Prayers

The writings of church mystics are filled with prayers that passionately express a love of Jesus Christ that is born out of his suffering and death upon the cross. An intense expression of this passion can be found in a prayer of the thirteenth-century saint Clare of Assisi, who wrote,

> Praise and glory be to you, O Loving Jesus Christ, for the most sacred wound in your side, and by that adorable wound and by your infinite mercy which you made known to us in the opening of your breast to the soldier Longinus, and so to us all. I pray you, O most gentle Jesus, having redeemed me by baptism from original sin, so now by your precious blood, which is offered and received throughout the world, deliver me from all evils, past, present, and to come. And, by your most bitter death give me a lively faith, a firm hope and a perfect charity, so that I may love you with all my heart and all my soul and all my strength; make me firm and

steadfast in good works and grant me perseverance in your service, so that I may be able to please you always. Amen.[1]

For Clare of Assisi, the wounds, blood, and death of Christ are expressions of the deep intimate love that her savior had displayed to her centuries earlier. She called the wounds of Christ "sacred" and "adorable," his blood "precious," and his death "most bitter," which is followed by her sweet desire for a "lively faith, a firm hope and a perfect charity," so that she might love Christ with all her heart and all her soul and all her strength in order to please him always.

The sixteenth-century saint Teresa of Avila expressed similar feelings of intimacy, also based upon the suffering and death of Christ upon the cross. She prayed,

> My God, because you are so good, I love you with all my heart, and for your sake I love my neighbor as myself. If I love you, it is not just because of heaven which you promised; if I fear to offend you, it is not because hell threatens me. What draws me to you, O Lord, is yourself alone, it is the sight of you, nailed to the cross for me, your body bruised in the pains of death. Your love so holds my heart that, if there were no heaven, I would love you still. If there were no hell I would even still fear to offend you. I do not need your gifts to make me love you, for even if I should have no help of hope at all the things I do hope for, I would still love you with that very same love.[2]

What draws out her deep love for Christ is the sight of him "nailed to the cross" and his "body bruised in the pains of death." She is so gripped by the painful love that Christ expressed that "so holds [her] heart" that "if there were no heaven" she would still love him and if "there were no hell" she would "still fear to offend" him. She culminates her feelings of love by stating that even if she should have no "hope at all [of] the things [she does] hope for," she would still love her savior with the very same love.

The intimate, passionate, and personal relationship these saints felt stemmed from their belief that the love Christ expressed through his death on the cross could be felt hundreds of years later. The sixteenth-century saint Francis Xavier unmistakably makes this point in the following prayer when he notes that the "bloody sweats" from "a thorny crown" that

---

1. In Dollen, ed., *Prayer Book of the Saints*, 84.
2. In Dollen, ed., *Prayer Book of the Saints*, 128–29.

Impassioned Spiritual Practices

"transpierced [Christ's] sacred brow" were expressions of love both in the past and in the present:

> O God, you are the object of my love, not for the hope of endless joys above, nor for the fear of endless pains below, which those who love you not must undergo. For me and such as me, you once did bear the ignominious cross, the nails, the spear; a thorny crown transpierced your sacred brow; what bloody sweats from every member flow. Such as then was and is your love for me, such is and shall be still my love for thee; Your love, O Jesus, will I ever sing—O God of love, sweet savior, dearest king.[3]

Of course, there are many other passionate love prayers by saints expressing the deep, intimate, and personal relationships they had with Christ. Not all the prayers explicitly describe the wounds, blood, and death of Jesus Christ. However, the prayers explicitly describe the mutually loving relationship the saints felt that is based upon the love that Christ expressed to all of humanity when he died on the cross and that he expresses to all of humanity today.

An urban monk may similarly pray,

> As I gaze upon you on the cross, please sharpen my passion to pierce the pettiness of prejudice and to perceive the beauty of true human solidarity. Guide my intellect to a meaningful understanding of the problems of the poor, of the oppressed, of the wounded, and all who bear the indignities of injustice and are in need of your love born out of your suffering and death upon the cross. Fill my heart with the fire of your love. May I hunger and thirst after justice always.

A Restless Night's Sleep

A restless night's sleep is not an intentional spiritual practice. We should, however, embrace it as a beneficial time to commune with God.

For an urban monk, restlessness before going to bed may be the result of yearning to help solve a social struggle that we are grappling with over time, and perhaps that very day while civically engaged.

Reflecting upon Scripture allows us a time to communicate with God. We can see this time as having someone we can express our feelings of restlessness to through our thoughts, which we believe God can hear as we lay wakeful upon our bed.

3. In Dollen, ed., *Prayer Book of the Saints*, 126–27.

If our restlessness becomes too intense, we may get out of bed and read Scripture as a way to verbally express our feelings to God. While reading Scripture, we may hear some of what we read as God responding to us.

I often have the experience of lying in bed at night filled with anxiety about a particular social struggle. Sometimes my anxiety speaks louder than my faith. A restless night's sleep can reflect a state in which we struggle with issues that we yearn to see resolved through spiritual intervention, as the writer of the Song of Solomon did:

> All night long on my bed
>   I looked for the one my heart loves;
>   I looked for him but did not find him.
> I will get up now and go about the city,
>   through its streets and squares;
> I will search for the one my heart loves.
>   So I looked for him but did not find him.
> The watchmen found me
>   as they made their rounds in the city.
>   "Have you seen the one my heart loves?"
> Scarcely had I passed them
>   when I found the one my heart loves.
> I held him and would not let him go
>   till I had brought him to my mother's house,
>   to the room of the one who conceived me.
> (Song of Solomon 3:1–4)

Our yearning becomes so strong on restless nights that we often get up and go about our homes as if they were the "streets and squares" of the city (v. 2). Late at night our home is different because there is little, if any, normal daytime activity. We can sit in silence and be surrounded by an outside darkness and an inside darkness if we so choose. We may vacillate between getting up and going about the "streets and squares" by pacing the floor or going from one room to the next, or just sitting on a chair or lying on a couch, as if God is saying, "Let him sit alone in silence, for the Lord has laid it on him" (Lam 3:28). In the midst of it all, we may feel anguish and shed tears for unknown reasons.

"Have you seen the one my heart loves?" is what we would want to ask if found suddenly by a watchman or someone else (v. 3). However, we may feel that we do not want to be disturbed by another, so instead we ask ourselves, "Have you seen the one my heart loves?" intermittently throughout this silent, lonely, and dark time.

Finding the "one my heart loves" and holding on to our lover and not letting go "till I had brought [my lover] to my mother's house, to the room of the one who conceived me" may or may not happen at the end of this late nighttime anxiety. Bringing God to your "mother's house" and into "the room of the one who conceived [you]" or simply back to your bed where the evening began is an intimacy we crave and can experience with God.

However, this is not always an experience of intimate warmth and peace. It may be a time of continued anxiety and other emotions. We may ask, "My soul is [still] in anguish. How long, O LORD, how long?" (Ps 6:3). We may also say to the one our heart loves, "I am worn out from groaning all night long and I drench[ed] my couch with tears" (Ps 6:6). And we may say to ourselves loud enough for our lover to hear, "My eyes grow weak with sorrow, and I grow weaker in your arms. Do not let me go" (Ps 6:7).

Dark Night of the Soul

St. John of the Cross has forever etched the descriptive words "dark night of the soul" into the spiritual heart of our world. The dark night of the soul is an ongoing experience of divine revelation. It is a place, as St. John notes, where God "nurtures and caresses [our] soul." That place, he notes, is "lengthy periods at prayer" or an "entire night" of awakening experiences that we all too often avoid.[4]

St. John of the Cross also tells us that the dark night is part of an awakening journey that is filled with constant experiences of darkness and death. Encounters with darkness are experiences of spiritual purgation; St. John calls them "rays of darkness." Darkness occurs when we are blinded by a brilliant light of divine opportunity such as loving God with all our heart and with all our soul and loving our neighbor as ourselves (Luke 10:27). Darkness also occurs when we are blinded by a brilliant light of divine illumination that reveals our own imperfections. St. John explains that death can occur daily if we allow it to happen. Dying to our own avoidance and shortcomings helps us to purge our own habitual ignorance and imperfections and move beyond our limited self to the self that lives eternally in God, both in time and beyond time.

The phrase "dark night of the soul" nonetheless has been used broadly by others over the centuries. Its most basic meaning has always been

---

4. Saint John of the Cross, *The Essential St. John of the Cross*, 373.

connected to a lengthy and profound absence of light and hope. In the dark night you feel profoundly alone.

Recent publications have described the dark night of the soul as a means of finding your way through life's ordeals, such as divorce, career disappointments, illnesses, substance abuse, codependency, and other such life struggles. Thus, some people tend to view the dark night of the soul in a more clinical sense—as threats to our well-being that we should attempt to overcome and heal from as quickly as possible. And when we are no longer distressed, distraught, or depressed, we should thank God that we have been restored and do everything we can to not wind up in a similar state of being.

However, St. John of the Cross describes the dark night of the soul more as a period of incubation during which an individual should delve into the soul's deepest needs in order to attain a deeper union with God. This is further achieved through more, and lengthy, "dark night of the soul" experiences. St. John explains that God leads us into such experiences to provide opportunity for spiritual progression and to transform our relationship with God.

I view the dark night of the soul as an opportunity to embrace some daily urban experiences that we so often shun. Doing so provides a means by which we can integrate our daily secular experiences to finding solutions to social injustice with our relationship with God and progress spiritually by purging things that are not Christlike.

We encounter many people daily that we all too often avoid out of feelings of discomfort or intolerance: people experiencing homelessness, the mentally ill, substance abusers, and victims of domestic violence. Such people may be begging for money, flailing their arms as they are talking to themselves, drinking alcohol in public, or hurriedly seeking shelter from an abuser. We may encounter day laborers, recyclers sifting through trash, street vendors, or loiterers.

To enter into a dark night of the soul is to embrace these daily experiences that we so often shun, then integrate them into our urban spiritual lives by allowing things that are not Christlike at first glance to become Christlike.

Embracing these daily occurrences allows a "dark night of the soul" experience to act as a mirror that can allow us to see ourselves in people we may avoid. We may feel we are one or two paychecks away from homelessness, or that there is some past traumatic event we have not fully dealt with. We may have a family member or friend who is struggling with mental illness or substance abuse. These daily experiences can also allow us to see God in these people who make us feel uncomfortable.

A dark night of a soul is not necessarily an encounter with God during which we want to overcome "negative" experiences as quickly as possible. Such experiences are not necessarily threats to our well-being that should be healed as quickly as possible.

St. John of the Cross portrays the dark night of the soul as a time of nurturing during which we should explore the depths of our soul out of a desire for a more profound union with God. He describes God as wanting to lead us into a dark night of the soul in order to experience divine revelation and transformative love. The dark night of the soul is a place where God "nurtures and caresses [our] soul" for an "entire night" if we so desire.

Such nurturance and affection help us to become willing to allow our own imperfections to die, an experience that moves us out of our ignorance and into the true self in God. Thus, it is not just a matter of increased knowledge or understanding. It is incarnating the truth that we received from God's involvement in our daily world. This takes time—perhaps even years—to develop fully.

Groaning

"Lord, I pray that your Spirit groan the words I do not even know how to pray when it concerns the homeless. Lord, I feel so powerless to actually help," I wrote and prayed at times.

At times you may likely feel the same. Committing to the life and work of an urban monk is to know the odds are stacked against you but to trust that God will provide the strength and focus to continue in service to the struggle. Including groaning as an impassioned practice in your integrated rule of life provides the time and place to bring these inevitable feelings of exhaustion and despair to God, even when you can't find the words to express them.

The spiritual practice of groaning is based upon the following scriptures that express a sense of helplessness when we do not know what to pray for and we need the Spirit to intercede through wordless groans. The Scriptures are filled with examples of people groaning in hopes of God hearing and interceding. For example:

> During that long period, the king of Egypt died. The Israelites groaned in their slavery and cried out, and their cry for help because of their slavery went up to God. God heard their groaning and he remembered his covenant with Abraham, with Isaac and

with Jacob. So God looked on the Israelites and was concerned about them. (Exod 2:23–24)

The following passage, however, describes "wordless groans" through which the Spirit intercedes for us during times of weakness. As we engage the Herculean task of finding solutions to challenging and complex social injustices day in and day out, we feel depleted, and we may feel that anything we say to God we've said before. In our helplessness we may begin groaning as an expression of disapproval, grief, and feeling overburdened:

> In the same way, the Spirit helps us in our weakness. For we do not know how we ought to pray, but the Spirit Himself intercedes for us with groans too deep for words. And He who searches our hearts knows the mind of the Spirit, because the Spirit intercedes for the saints according to the will of God. (Rom 8:26–27)

Psalm 12:5 reads "'Because the poor are plundered and the needy groan, I will now arise,' says the LORD. 'I will protect them from those who malign them.'" This reminds us that God will "arise" because of the needy's groans. "The needy" is synonymous with those in poverty. In the case of the urban monk facing despair in the face of social ills and issues, we are the needy experiencing a poverty of words, and God will arise in response to our groans to offer comfort and spiritual renewal.

Reflection Questions

- What are the Scripture passages, prayers, speeches, stories, quotes, or forms of art you have used that go beyond the structure and instruction of your discipline practices to fuel an increasing inner passion to help right a social wrong?
- When you think about the social struggle that you have committed to, what feelings do you experience that might be described as "passionate"?
- How might your passionate emotions benefit you in your work to find solutions for your social struggle?
- When have your passionate emotions worked against you or hindered your progress?
- When in the past has a "dark night of the soul" experience been a source of healing rather than something to endure?

8

Merging the Sacred and the Secular for Social Action

The main thing is never to get discouraged at the slowness of people or results. People may not be articulate or active, but even so, we do not ever know the results, or the effect on souls. That is not for us to know. We can only go ahead and work with happiness at what God sends us to do.

—Dorothy Day

WE DEVELOP A RULE of life by choosing a social struggle to commit to and choosing biblically rooted spiritual principles and practices to help guide and nourish us as we carry out this challenging work. We live our rule of life when we apply those spiritual principles and practices to our secular life, specifically to our efforts to help find solutions to social injustices and bring healing to the world, starting with our own community.

In this chapter I share some ways that I live out my rule of life as a fulcrum for social action, specifically to the social struggle of homelessness. You will see how I engage some of my chosen spiritual principles and practices in the secular world with the goal of enacting lasting social reform. While not all of it will speak to your life, I hope in it you will find inspiration to further develop and evolve your rule of life, to stay committed to your chosen struggle, and to deepen your spiritual life and relationship with God.

"I Give You My Word"

One of the most precious gifts that we can give to others is our "word." To say to someone, "I give you my word" can be one of the most sacred gifts you can give to an individual or community.

As a young boy, I knew that a sense of sacredness surrounded the utterance "I give you my word." Each Christmas I heard the good news that God has given us God's Word—Christ. During the holiday we celebrate the giving of the word of God and the fulfillment of God's Word: "For no word from God will ever fail," the angel Gabriel said to Mary (Luke 1:37).

"Here is my servant, whom I uphold, my chosen one in whom I delight; I will put my Spirit on him, and he will bring justice to the nations" is a prophetic reference to the word of God (Isa 42:1). Matthew wrote that Christ was the fulfillment of God's word spoken through the prophet Isaiah (Matt 12:18).

"Your word, O LORD, is everlasting; it is firmly fixed in the heavens," cried the psalmist (Ps 119:89), and the prophet Isaiah declared, "The grass withers and the flowers fall, but the word of our God endures forever" (Isa 40:8). The apostle Peter proclaimed, "All people are like grass, and all their glory is like the flowers of the field; the grass withers and the flowers fall but the word of the Lord endures forever. And this word is the good news that was preached to you" (1 Pet 1:24–25).

As I grew up, I began to sense more and more the seriousness of saying to someone "I give you my word" when I wanted to assure the person I really meant that I was going to carry out the action I had just promised. It felt more like a vow than simply a promise. There were times when, right after I emphatically said to someone, "I give you my word," I said to myself, "Should I have said it? I now have no choice but to carry out my word. I want to, but can I really do it?"

As urban monks, we can emphatically say to someone or to a community, "I give you my word," and then we carry out the promise out of a sense of sacredness. After giving our sacred word, we can "let the word of Christ dwell in [us] richly" (Col 3:16) and reflect upon, and internally echo, the following sacred words of God:

> My word that proceeds from my mouth will not return to me empty, but it will accomplish what I please, and it will prosper where I send it. (Isa 55:11)

Merging the Sacred and the Secular for Social Action

We can all turn to someone who is physically or emotionally pained and say, "I give you my word that I will be there for you, I will support you, I will stand by your side." We can all turn to a community and say likewise, "You can count on me." And the most precious and deeply felt gift we can receive in return is hearing God say, "[You are] my servant, whom I uphold, my chosen one in whom I delight."

As urban monks, it is important that we uphold the sacredness of our word in all our actions. Our integrated rule of life is a good place to document this commitment: the grass may wither and the flowers may die but not our given word.

Embracing the Arc of the Moral Universe

I first heard about "bending the arc of the moral universe" in high school. I did not become familiar with the virtue until I became increasingly involved in trying to help solve social struggles, which included reading and learning about how social reformers had tried to do the same.

A moral universe implies that we live in a spiritual universe as opposed to a purely physical one, or one in which there is no moral force and thus no consequence to our actions. A moral universe forms the basis of compassion, altruism, and charity, which reaches into the lives of people and our neighborhoods, cities, and states. This arc can even reach into the lives of entire nations.

Renowned social reformers have noted that an arc rooted in compassion and charity can bend toward justice. Theodore Parker, the nineteenth-century social reformer and abolitionist, predicted the inevitable success of the abolitionist cause to end slavery in the US when he stated,

> I do not pretend to understand the moral universe; the arc is a long one, my eye reaches but little ways; I cannot calculate the curve and complete the figure by the experience of sight; I can divine it by conscience. And from what I see I am sure it bends towards justice.[1]

A century later, Martin Luther King Jr. paraphrased these words to great effect in his famous "Where Do We Go from Here?" speech during the 1967 Southern Christian Leadership Conference: "The arc of the moral universe is long, but it bends toward justice."

---

1. Parker, *Ten Sermons of Religion*, 84–85.

Less than a year later, he said it again in a speech at the National Cathedral in Washington, DC: "We shall overcome because the arc of the moral universe is long, but it bends toward justice."

These are not the only times that Dr. King employed these words. As he was ending his sermon "Why I Am Opposed to the War in Vietnam" at the Ebenezer Baptist Church in 1967, he remarked,

> And I have not lost faith. I'm not in despair, because I know that there is a moral order. I haven't lost faith, because the arc of the moral universe is long, but it bends toward justice. I can still sing "We Shall Overcome" because Carlyle was right: "No lie can live forever." We shall overcome because William Cullen Bryant was right: "Truth pressed to earth will rise again." We shall overcome because James Russell Lowell was right: "Truth forever on the scaffold, wrong forever on the throne." Yet, that scaffold sways the future. We shall overcome because the Bible is right: "You shall reap what you sow."

He used these words again at the end of the series of marches from Selma, Alabama, to Montgomery, which brought the civil rights movement to a political height. The first march was known as Bloody Sunday because the marchers were beaten by law enforcement officers. The violence was recorded and televised, resulting in greater public support of the civil rights movement. The second march, which occurred a couple of days later, ended after the marchers were again confronted by law enforcement. The third march had the right of a court order allowing for it and took five days, with the marchers averaging ten miles a day. At the end of the third march on March 25, 1965, Dr. King stood on the steps of the state capital and delivered his "How Long, Not Long" speech to nearly thirty thousand people. As he wound down his speech, Dr. King proclaimed,

> I come to say to you this afternoon, however difficult the moment, however frustrating the hour, it will not be long, because "truth crushed to earth will rise again."
>
> How long? Not long, because "no lie can live forever."
>
> How long? Not long, because "you shall reap what you sow."
>
> How long? Not long:
> Truth forever on the scaffold,
> Wrong forever on the throne,

Merging the Sacred and the Secular for Social Action

> Yet that scaffold sways the future,
> And, behind the dim unknown,
> Standeth God within the shadow,
> Keeping watch above his own.
> How long? Not long,
> because the arc of the moral universe is long,
> but it bends toward justice.

The work of the urban monk contributes to the force that bends the universe in a moral direction. The more urban monks commit to finding solutions to social injustice, the more pressure is applied. Your rule of life is the place to document your progress as a reminder of what helps drive and sustain you as you do your part.

Integrating Scripture, Social Capital, and Social Reform

When I first started out as an urban monk, my efforts largely resulted in attempts to solve the problem of homelessness through charitable works. I had chosen a worthy cause and I wanted to act out of the goodness of my heart, but my actions were mostly limited to giving money if I had spare change and getting involved in hands-on ways if I had spare time.

While this was a good place to start, and charitable acts are essential components in the work to solve social injustice, I came to realize that my charitable acts were only Band-Aids; they wouldn't lead to widespread social reform and, ultimately, justice.

Justice is a matter of moral responsibility, according to many verses of Scripture, and is focused on changing a whole neighborhood or community, not just an individual. It requires us to do all we can, no matter the cost, and extends well beyond giving spare time or money.

Achieving justice requires social capital, a network of relationships we create with like-minded people that helps us achieve our goals in implementing social reform. The common elements of a social capital network include the social, economic, and moral resources of the people within the network—for example, money (cash, grants, etc.), property (low-rent apartment buildings, empty storefronts to use outreach centers, etc.), and goodwill among the people and organizations that make up the network to disseminate those resources. Thus, social capital comprises both the network and the assets that may be mobilized through that network.

The Way of the Urban Monk

Our faith guides us regarding the root of our abundance and our drive to share it: "The earth is the LORD's, and everything in it, the world, and all who live in it" (Ps 24:1). In Psalm 84:1 the psalmist exclaims that "the heavens are yours, and yours also the earth; you founded the world and all that is in it" (Ps 89:11). The New Testament echoes these very words: "The earth is the Lord's, and everything in it" (1 Cor 10:26).

When we fail to acknowledge that all our assets and resources belong to God and when we withhold any resources that God has given us to share with others, we begin a cycle of spiritual poverty and risk a deteriorating relationship with God. However, when we share our resources that God has given us within a network, they increased manyfold.

> As it is written: "He has scattered abroad His gifts to the poor; His righteousness endures forever." Now He who supplies seed to the sower and bread for food will supply and multiply your store of seed and will increase the harvest of your righteousness. (2 Cor 9:10–11)

Every urban monk, regardless of their chosen social struggle, should draft that wisdom into their rule of life and carry it with them into their work.

Scriptures also help guide us in choosing to whom we direct the resources of our collective action. For example, as mentioned in an earlier chapter, the Psalms state that God wants justice administered to the following people:

- the oppressed (9:9; 10:12; 103:6; 146:7)
- the orphan (10:17; 68:5; 82:3; 146:9)
- the poor (12:5; 41:1; 72:4, 12; 140:12)
- the needy (12:5; 72:4, 12; 82:4; 109:31; 140:12)
- the widows (68:5; 146:9)
- the desolate (68:6; 82:3)
- the weak (72:12; 82:3)
- the hungry (107:9; 146:7)
- the brokenhearted (147:3)

I have been moved to fulfill these commands by integrating Scripture while seeking to administer justice as directed by God. For example, reading the book of Isaiah and thus hearing God say, "Maintain justice, and do what is right" (Isa 56:1a) or "Learn to do right; seek justice. Defend the oppressed. Take up the cause of the fatherless; plead the case of the widow" (Isa 1:17). What has been particularly moving for me has been reading and thus hearing God say, "Here is my servant, whom I uphold, my chosen in whom my soul delights; I have put my Spirit upon him, he will bring forth justice to the nations" (Isa 42:1).

For me, this is perhaps the most moving of all verses in Isaiah:

> So justice is driven back,
>   and righteousness stands at a distance;
> truth has stumbled in the streets,
>   honesty cannot enter.
> Truth is nowhere to be found,
>   and whoever shuns evil becomes a prey.
> The LORD looked and was displeased
>   that there was no justice.
> He saw that there was no one,
>   he was appalled that there was no one to intervene. (Isa 59:14–16)

When I read this passage, I want God to see me as someone who wants to intervene. I have the same reaction when I read Ezekiel 22:30:

> I looked for someone among them who would build up the wall
> and stand before me in the gap on behalf of the land
> so I would not have to destroy it, but I found no one.

I want God to find me willing to stand in the gap on behalf of the land. And I have learned that I can do this from within my social network, as part of a collective group. The collective groups I've been part of over the years have focused on affordable housing, small business development, and homelessness. Homelessness in particular is tied to other issues such as chronic health conditions, disabilities, domestic violence, incarceration, limited income, mental illness, and substance abuse.

Together we leverage and coordinate the assets and resources of a wide range of public and private agencies, committees, groups, and organizations to administer justice. Among us are businesses, corporations, civic groups, faith-based organizations, local government, and nonprofit agencies. Being part of such a network has helped me shift from a charitable approach to "serving" a social injustice to committing to *solving* it, which has a specific and desired outcome—social reform. Only collectively can such complex issues of social injustice be solved.

Building a network of social capital in order to seek justice for the homeless has helped me move beyond self-interest—what I get out of my involvement through acts of charity—to collective interest. Shifting from individual to collective interest has helped me focus on what *we* get out of it, knowing that what is good for the neighborhood or community is good for all of us.

To be truly effective, Christians—and congregations—must be willing to act with local government, civic organizations, secular individuals, and congregations of different faiths with the shared goal of enacting lasting social reform. Guided by their rule of life, urban monks can be models for successfully merging the sacred and the secular to find solutions for social injustice.

Integrating the Spiritual and Social Aspects of Prayer and Piety

Jesus, of course, is our best model for spirituality as a driving force of righteous change in the secular world. When asked, "Teacher, which commandment is the greatest in the Law?" (Matt 22:36), Christ did not sever the spiritual and social aspects of prayer and piety but connected them. He declared,

> "Love the Lord your God with all your heart and with all your soul and with all your mind." This is the first and greatest commandment. And the second is like it: "Love your neighbor as yourself." All the Law and the Prophets depend on these two commandments. (Matt 22:37–40)

Earlier in the Gospel of Matthew, Jesus is approached by a man who asks, "Teacher, what good thing must I do to get eternal life?" Jesus replies, "If you want to enter life, keep the commandments." The man asks, "Which ones?" After listing several of them, Jesus ends the list with "Love your neighbor as yourself" (Matt 19:16–18).

Prayer, piety, and efforts to end social injustice are integrated when we obey the "first and greatest commandment" and the second one to "love your neighbor as yourself." We put faith into action; we take our spiritual principles and practices into our community. This integrated action nurtures an intimate, personal, and private relationship with God and cultivates collective relationship with God and our neighbors—our family, friends, coworkers, students, congregations, neighbors, organizations, community groups, acquaintances, and even the strangers who live among us. As it reads in the first epistle of John, "Anyone who loves God must also love their brother and sister" (1 John 4:21).

Anyone who participates in organizing the efforts and resources of a community knows that relationships are not always easy. Our counties, cities, and communities—often via committees, commissions, and coalitions representing various jurisdictions—frequently present problems and prepare plans to solve social issues and ills that perplex people. The problems they address are often long-standing and broad reaching: blight, congestion, crime, discrimination, homelessness, poverty, prejudice, sickness, trash, underemployment and unemployment; the plans are often highly complex.

I've learned through my work with homelessness that personal piety can help us nurture and navigate these community relationships. The English word *piety* is derived from the Latin word *pietas*, which is understood as an expression of love and loyalty toward God, but it also means an expression of love and loyalty toward our fellow human beings, which I found helpful when participating in civic and community planning to help solve social struggles.

Social plans include civic planning that involves drafting general plans, specific plans, and master plans, which are often products of committees, commissions, and coalitions—people working closely together with shared goals but also personal agendas. Piety—especially the commandment to "love our neighbor as ourselves" (Luke 10:27)—has proved fortifying for me in all stages of this kind of work and community building in my efforts to find solutions for homelessness.

General Plans

General plans are often a city's overarching policy statement based on community decision-making concerning future residential, commercial, and recreational development. Housing, economic policy, parks and open space, transportation, safety, community design, and conservation of natural resources are included, allowing community participants to help shape solutions to problems such as affordable housing, unemployment/underemployment, lack of open space, traffic and pedestrian accidents, and neighborhood disinvestment.

Specific Plans

Specific plans are similar to general plans but focus on a particular area or neighborhood within a city. Community decision-making is often made by those living within the specific area or neighborhood. As I like to remind myself and my team members in this work, drafting a specific plan provides a special opportunity to love one's neighbor as oneself by brainstorming solutions to the problems that we share with our next-door neighbor or those living on the same street.

Master Plans

Master plans can focus on an institution that you may be involved with. I am adjunct faculty at Fuller Theological Seminary located in Pasadena, California. During the 1980s, the seminary wanted to clear its campus of several buildings to build more student housing. The city asked the seminary for a master plan, essentially a map—designed in part by the affected community—that shapes the future development of the campus. As a result, many of the existing buildings were preserved and are used today as offices, conference rooms, and classrooms. Today, the seminary has a master plan as well as an expanded library. Community decision-making continues.

Community Plans

Community plans are often products of committees, commissions, and coalitions that describe social struggles and solutions to end them. Committees, commissions, and coalitions are usually formed to facilitate decision-making among stakeholders.

During the 1990s, I was involved in many community plans that dealt with fair housing issues. I was the primary writer for more than twenty fair housing plans and reports for various cities in Los Angeles and neighboring counties. The plans were mandated by the US Department of Housing and Urban Development (HUD). In their initial planning guide, HUD acknowledged that

> communities were not involved in the decision-making process, and what started out as instruments of principle became rules of process that were to be minimized or even ignored. The result has been a failure by many communities to embrace their legal and

Merging the Sacred and the Secular for Social Action

moral obligation to ensure that people are not denied housing opportunity in that community because of their race, ethnic origin, religion, disability, or the fact that they are a family with children.[2]

Where was the piety—loving our neighbors as ourselves—in that? The plans that I helped shape for each of the cities pulled together data to show if there were any discriminatory practices in housing. The plans also noted what activities to undertake to correct the malpractices. For example, potential renters were denied housing because of their ethnic origin, disability, or because they had too many children. Recommendations included training and workshops to educate property managers and owners about fair housing practices, or in some cases, when offenses were egregious, lawsuits. Another example concerned land use. Cities would require conditional use permits (CUPs) if an apartment building was designated for formerly homeless people, but the same building was permitted by right if designated for others who had not experienced homelessness. In these instances, recommendations to ensure fair housing implementation included zoning code changes by cities to remove such practices.

During the last decade, I was involved in writing several community plans known as ten-year plans to end homelessness. At the beginning of the decade, in 2010, homelessness in the United States had become deeply rooted and there were no signs that the problem was lessening, let alone ending. By the end of the decade, this seemingly intractable problem of homelessness saw unprecedented decreases in the number of people experiencing homelessness as these plans were implemented. Leadership was provided at the national level through the US Interagency Council on Homelessness, which stimulated leadership at the local jurisdictional level. Evidence-based and best practices were introduced to a wide range of local stakeholders who were encouraged to adapt and/or adopt the practices that still are actively promoted today. Most notably, homelessness among veterans has continued to decrease significantly.

---

2. U.S. Department of Housing and Urban Development Office of Fair Housing and Equal Opportunity, *Fair Housing Planning Guide*, Vol. 1, i.

Zoning Codes, Conditional Use Permits, and Unconditional Love

Public hearings, which are a key part of the approval process in a request for a conditional use permit (CUP) as outlined in zoning codes, have often become contentious and combative when the conditional use of residential buildings focuses on the people who will live in them. I have witnessed this over and over again during the past twenty years when the approval process shifted away from development standards—the original intent of the approval process—to "unwanted" people with physical and/or developmental disabilities and others who were homeless at the time. You may have witnessed the same thing in similar settings.

The typical zoning code identifies the uses of land for each zoning district, which generally includes residential, open-space, commercial, and industrial zones. Development standards for specific land uses are also identified and typically include lot size, lot coverage, setbacks, height limits, and parking requirements. Residential land use commonly includes single-family and multi-family housing, which are permitted by right and do not require a conditional use permit.

A conditional use permit allows property owners to use their buildings in ways that are not otherwise permitted within the zone in which the property is located. For example, the first floor of a corner building in a residential neighborhood may be conditionally permitted to be used as a small grocery store while the upper floor is used as a residence.

Conditional use permits allow property owners to use their land and buildings in many other ways that are not permitted in the same zone. Houses within commercial zones have been allowed to become offices and their backyards to become concrete-covered parking lots. Churches, schools, restaurants, and many other land uses have been conditionally permitted in zoning districts that at one time did not allow such uses.

Conditional use permit requests are required when property owners have proposed to use their buildings for housing for people with disabilities and for those who are homeless; a conditional use permit is required when the land use is not considered single-family or multi-family housing. In such cases the land use is considered a group home, typically defined as a planned single housekeeping unit that provides care and supervision for a limited number of residents who, although unrelated, live together as a family unit. The care and supervision are nonmedical apart from dispensing prescribed medications.

Merging the Sacred and the Secular for Social Action

The approval of a conditional use permit request requires public hearing notices. Usually, all property owners within 300 feet of the site for which a conditional use permit request is submitted receive a notice regarding the public hearing. Public hearings are officiated by a zoning hearing officer whose job is to determine whether the proposed conditional use will materially alter the surrounding neighborhood and, if so, whether the change will have a negative or positive impact.

The zoning hearing officer usually keeps the focus on the physical impacts of the proposed use, such as adequate parking, front yard setbacks, building separation, height limits, and so forth. Participants in the process often focus on the negative impacts of the people who will live in the building, particularly when the use is intended to be a group home for low-income people. I have seen participants raise parking or front yard setback requirements as issues in hopes that such requirements would not be met and consequently prevent "certain people" from living in a building.

It is at this point that practicing piety becomes especially challenging. In such a setting, loving one another as yourself means providing a voice for the voiceless and allowing people to express their negative feelings—allowing everyone to be heard and seen.

In such community engagement, I draw on unconditional love, a foundational principle in my rule of life. This is a love without conditions or circumstances, as noted throughout the New Testament. Romans 13:10 tells us, "Love does no wrong to its neighbor." First Peter 3:8 guides us to "be like-minded, be sympathetic, love one another, be compassionate and humble." Ephesians 4:2 advises, "Be completely humble and gentle; be patient, bearing with one another in love."

Unconditional love particularly dominates the actions, teachings, and prayers of Christ right before his crucifixion. The apostle John writes about these final hours:

> It was just before the Passover Festival. Jesus knew that the hour had come for him to leave this world and go to the Father. Having loved his own who were in the world, he loved them to the end. (John 13:1)

After washing his disciples' feet, Jesus exclaims,

> Do you understand what I have done for you? . . . You call me "Teacher" and "Lord," and rightly so, for that is what I am. Now that I, your Lord and Teacher, have washed your feet, you also should wash one another's feet. I have set you an example that you

should do as I have done for you. Very truly I tell you, no servant is greater than his master, nor is a messenger greater than the one who sent him. Now that you know these things, you will be blessed if you do them. (John 13:12b–17)

After Jesus predicts his betrayal and right before to tells Peter that "before the rooster crows, you will disown me three times," he tells his disciples,

> A new commandment I give you: Love one another.
> As I have loved you, so also you must love one another.
> By this (everyone) will know that you are my disciples, if you love one another. (John 13:34–35)

Later, while praying in the garden, shortly before his arrest, Christ ends his prayer for his disciples and for us today by praying "Righteous Father, . . . I have made you known to them, and will continue to make you known in order that the love you have for me may be in them and that I myself may be in them" (John 17:26).

Allowing the love of Christ in us to manifest itself will overcome any challenges we may feel about neighbors who have a disability or may have been homeless. In the case of my work with homelessness, loving our neighbors means ensuring that development standards are in place so that group homes remain in character with other homes in terms of design, health, and safety. Focusing on such development standards helps community members who express negative feelings—who are opposed to the group homes—feel seen and heard, that our unconditional love isn't solely focused on the people who will be living in the group homes.

As briefly mentioned earlier, allowing the love of Christ within us to manifest itself means reaching everyone. Public hearings concerning group homes are often not attended by those who will reside in the homes. Thus, they may be voiceless. When this happens, I summon my unconditional love for them, guided by the Old Testament's wisdom to "speak up for those who cannot speak for themselves, for the rights of all who are destitute. Speak up and judge fairly; defend the rights of the poor and needy" (Prov 31:8–9).

Just hours before his death and a few days before his resurrection, Christ says to his disciples, "I have kept my Father's commands." The implication is that so should we.

> As the Father has loved me, so have I loved you. Now remain in my love. If you keep my commands, you will remain in my love,

just as I have kept my Father's commands and remain in his love. I have told you this so that my joy may be in you and that your joy may be complete. My command is this: Love each other as I have loved you. (John 15:9–12)

Including unconditional love as part of our rule of life will help us with this. It will help us see that every public hearing is an opportunity to express unconditional love so that Christ's joy may be in us, and our joy may be complete. We reach out and represent those we serve with this love and encourage them to do the same. As Dorothy Day writes,

> Love and ever more love is the only solution to every problem that comes up. If we love each other enough, we will bear with each other's faults and burdens. If we love enough, we are going to light that fire in the hearts of others. And it is love that will burn out the sins and hatreds that sadden us. It is love that will make us want to do great things for each other. No sacrifice and no suffering will then seem too much.[3]

Streets and Sidewalks: The Real and the Ideal

Perhaps, like me, you have reflected on the following Old Testament words as a source for inspiration, especially if you have ventured into issues related to community and economic development: "You will be called repairer of broken walls, restorer of streets with dwellings" (Isa 58:12). That is certainly a suitable epithet for any urban monk dedicated to finding solutions to complex social problems.

In my experience as an urban monk committed to finding solutions to homelessness, living out these words over the years has made it clear that in many urban settings, the real and the ideal are often in conflict when it comes to streets and sidewalks. When uptown, downtown, old town, new town, or other areas become the focus of revitalization efforts, plans and drawings focusing on streets and sidewalks illuminate the ideal. Plans visualize ideal ways for people to walk, talk, and sit together. Facade improvements for buildings often include connecting the inside of buildings to the outside sidewalks and streets through large windows and glass doors to attract people passing by. Public art is usually integrated along with some greenery such as trees and plants. Of course, every pedestrian looks happy,

---

3. Day et al., *House of Hospitality*, 267.

and if drivers in cars were depicted in detail, they would all have smiles on their faces.

The real is frequently different from the ideal. On those actual streets and sidewalks may be people peddling illegal drugs and documents or panhandling. Vendors may be intrusively affecting the flow of traffic by selling fruits, vegetables, drinks, and candies up and down the middle of the roadways. Sex workers may be hailing drivers or greeting pedestrians. People may be rolling out blankets to sell goods along the sidewalk and to sleep. People with mental health issues may be flailing their arms and shouting or sitting on public benches or ledges talking to no one directly.

Urban monks—that is, repairers of broken walls and restorers of streets with dwellings—are often involved in working with various public and private agencies within a secular sphere: local government, businesses, business associations, neighborhood groups, and other civic organizations. Some Christians may be hesitant to do so because the church has historically been seen as a divinely instituted alternative to the secular world. While some congregations are not afraid to engage in good works in the secular world, for others the prevailing feeling may be that congregations live within the sphere of the sacred and need not be overly concerned about or involved in the secular. These congregations often view themselves as a place of social retreat and refuge from society's social struggles. Streets and sidewalks are just paths to get to church, work, home, and recreation.

In my experience working with others to end homelessness, joining with representatives from public and private agencies to change the real to the ideal can at first feel awkward and antithetical to well-intended goals of positive, practical, and profitable uses of streets and sidewalks. For some it may feel awkward simply because they don't have much experience working together in social contexts with elected or appointed officials, law enforcement, planners, building inspectors, architects, chambers of commerce, nonprofit organizations, and so forth. It can feel especially awkward for those who are there to try to help those people who are not using the streets and sidewalks for presumably positive and practical reasons. Their goals seemingly clash with those who don't seem to be promoting compassionate and constructive responses or who are proposing interventions that seem harsh and at times outright cruel. In the case of homelessness, this might look like efforts to displace panhandlers and criminalizing their behavior if they do not relocate.

Merging the Sacred and the Secular for Social Action

You may witness elected and appointed officials appearing to compromise their views and shift their positions for the sake of reaching consensus. But you may feel strongly about not compromising your own views, especially in the aftermath of watching others compromise their "secular" positions.

In the case of homelessness, I have seen people struggle to support proposals that are harsh toward aggressive panhandlers or those selling food items in the middle of streets instead of along sidewalks, as well as proposals that include severe treatment of people sleeping on the streets during the day. I have seen members of faith communities struggle with allowing congregations to pass out food along sidewalks and street corners or open spaces bordering them, such as parks and empty lots, without permits or permission. And I've seen people oppose proposals that do not allow preaching along streets and sidewalks, or those that allow preaching but not the use of amplifying equipment.

As a factor in your integrated rule of life, setting the goal to be a repairer of broken walls and a restorer of streets with dwellings can be the real deal. The journey to get there may not initially appear so, but it is. Hearing the diverse viewpoints of others may feel threatening to your own. Daring to reflect on such viewpoints may feel even more threatening. Of course, you will never know the outcome unless you enter the struggling world between the real and the ideal, which you may find, to your delight, to be sacred ground and not so secular after all.

Ridicule, Resistance, and Reconciliation in Ending Homelessness

In your work as an urban monk, you will inevitably face ridicule of your efforts and resistance to your belief that there are solutions to the most challenging and long-standing social injustices. In my experience, I have often been met with ridicule and resistance while working with others to end homelessness.

By ridicule, I mean sniggering—at times even laughter and outright mockery—often accompanied by sarcastic comments like, "Great goal," "Let's do it," "Sure thing," and "Definitely." The underlying idea is that ending homelessness is never going to happen. Mockery is more overt, the tone more accentuated. Phrases like "Get real" and "Get serious" are used.

Resistance includes continuing to participate in activities and services that have limited or no effect on ending homelessness. Such efforts include passing out food or serving meals in a park, giving spare change to people standing on the corner asking for money, and calling upon law enforcement to mitigate loitering and sleeping in public places.

Often, I have heard people paraphrasing Matthew 26:11, "The poor you will always have with you." I would immediately assert, "But they do not have to be homeless."

The paraphrased scripture seems to justify a fatalistic belief that by divine decree there will always be homeless people, that some people must be homeless in order to help fulfill Scripture and have no role to play in efforts to respond to their homelessness. I would often hear, "They want to be homeless." I would then hear, "They do not want to take the necessary steps to end their homelessness." Over and over, I heard people say that the homeless do not want to follow the rules to stay in a shelter, they do not want to give up alcohol and drugs, and they do not want to get a job.

The reality of such ridicule and resistance is precisely why reconciliation is a key aspect of my integrated rule of life. Reconciliation can follow ridicule and resistance when enough people who ridicule or resist ending homelessness join with those who believe we can end it. As the Roman Catholic priest Raimon Panikkar explains,

> Forgiveness, reconciliation, ongoing dialogue, lead to peace, a peace that is a way forward, not backward, for any return to a status-quo ante is a pipe dream. In order to forgive, to dialogue, to establish reconciliation one needs a strength beyond the mechanical order of action and reaction. One needs the Holy Spirit, *karuna*, *charis*, and love realized as being the pillars of the universe.
> To save humanity we have to become human.[4]

I have helped initiate reconciliation by explaining how homelessness can end in a community if the focus is on ending homelessness for a given subpopulation, such as seniors aged sixty-two or older, veterans, or youth aged eighteen to twenty-four.

As I mentioned in an earlier chapter, over the years I have helped coordinate homeless counts, which the US Department of Housing and Urban Development (HUD) requires from Continuums of Care to receive more than $1 billion in grant funds each year from HUD. Continuums of Care are regional organizations comprising a wide range of public and private partners that work together to end local homelessness. The State of California, for example, is divided into forty-four Continuums of Care.

---

4. Franck, Roze, and Connolly, *What Does It Mean to Be Human?*, 63.

Merging the Sacred and the Secular for Social Action

Homeless counts involve having an adequate number of volunteers count individuals who are homeless and gather demographic information that includes age, ethnicity, gender, race, health status, and veteran status, among other characteristics.

My involvement has included not only helping to methodologically coordinate the counts but also submitting a final report that includes an analysis of the collected data and recommendations regarding preventing and ending local homelessness. My analysis would also always include a breakdown of the data by each city within the geographic region of the Continuum of Care. The breakdown of the data for each city would include the total number of people counted who were living on the streets and their demographic information. Local stakeholders were challenged to end local homelessness.

Breaking down the total number of people would invite and initiate reconciliation. For example, if five hundred people were counted as unsheltered in a given city, a challenge to local stakeholders to help end homelessness for all five hundred people would likely come across as daunting and perhaps invite ridicule and resistance.

But reconciliation was the result when the total number of five hundred people was broken down further. Of the five hundred people, for example, 10 percent may be seniors ages sixty-two and older, and another 10 percent might be youth ages eighteen to twenty-four. Five percent may be veterans. Focusing on a smaller subset of the total number makes the challenge more manageable.

I have also invited and initiated reconciliation by helping local stakeholders understand the impact of trauma on people living on the streets. Homelessness itself is a traumatic experience. In fact, many people experiencing homelessness are likely suffering the effects of cumulative traumatic experiences lived in childhood or throughout their lifespan, including the events precipitating or leading up to homelessness. The cumulative effect of traumatic experiences has left many a person languishing on the streets and in a constant state of survival.

Reconciliation has happened when critical mass is achieved. Critical mass looks like the minimum number of local stakeholders needed to end the homelessness experience of fifty seniors ages sixty-two and older living on the streets of their city, or twenty-five veterans.

These local stakeholders understand that the lasting effects of trauma and the fear of being retraumatized may cause too many of the seniors or veterans to choose living in a constant state of survival on the streets rather than confronting the steps necessary to get off the streets, as counterintuitive as it may seem. They understand that these seniors and veterans need to know that a critical mass of people will be there for them as they shift from living in one-day-at-a-time survival mode to taking the actions necessary over days and weeks to obtain and maintain permanent housing.

Ridicule and resistance can give way to reconciliation. As I've seen my work, a critical mass of people, including those experiencing homelessness, can overcome seemingly irreconcilable perceptions and positions in order to mutually work together to help right a social wrong.

A Lasting Source of Strength

As you have seen throughout this chapter, the spiritual principles and practices included in your rule of life can and will have practical applications in your efforts to find solutions to your chosen social struggle. They will support you in community forums where you work with others to create plans to reach your goals. They will guide you as you serve on coalitions, committees, commissions, and councils specifically focused on your chosen social struggle and how it affects your neighborhood, community, city, and state. They will help you tap into a social capital network that includes social, economic, and moral resources that can be mobilized to right social wrongs. They will also help you tap into your piety and find your inner source of unconditional love as you navigate all levels of the secular world, including ridicule, resistance, and reconciliation. And, as I did, you will find that world to be receptive.

Reflection Questions

- As you work to help solve social struggles, when do you experience your spiritual principles in action?
- How do your spiritual practices support you in your efforts to find solutions for social injustice?
- What social capital have you developed that has helped you to merge the sacred and the secular to find solutions to social struggles?
- When have you felt that your reconciling efforts with others were met with ridicule and resistance? How did you handle it?

Merging the Sacred and the Secular for Social Action

- When have you had opportunities to express unconditional love while civically engaged?
- When and how have you been a voice for the voiceless?

9

Leaving a Lasting Spiritual Legacy

Entrust to reliable people who will also be qualified to teach others.

—2 Timothy 2:2

Leaving a lasting spiritual legacy continues to be an experience that I get to treasure over and over again. In my classes, my students are required to submit a final reflection paper detailing their integrated rule of life and the spiritual principles and practices they've chosen to include. I have had many former students request to meet because they wanted to share how what they learned from me changed the trajectory of their life.

They shared what they have been doing since they took my class, usually five or ten years ago. Not only did they become involved in the political life of their communities but a few of them also campaigned to be elected officials, such as a city council member and a superior court judge. Others were appointed by elected officials to a commission or committee and encouraged to participate in coalitions to help solve a local community issue. Some students chose to work for public entities such as counties and cities or private entities such as nonprofit organizations. During my meetings with them, we continue to talk about an integrated rule of life and leaving a lasting spiritual legacy.

Over the coming years and decades, your integrated rule of life will develop and evolve into a potent personal tool to help you in your efforts to solve seemingly intractable social struggles and deepen your relationship with God. But its guidance can carry on beyond your lifetime, serving as a torch to help others find their way in their efforts to solve social injustices.

Live It

One of the most powerful ways you can ensure that your integrated rule of life serves as a beacon for future generations is to live it and treat it as a living, growing, strengthening organism. The spiritual principles and practices you use to nurture an intimate, personal, and private relationship with God will likely increase, and those that you continue to use year after year will continuously mature your relationship with God. Your desire to have a deeply committed and intimate relationship with God will be progressively fulfilled with each passing year.

You will heighten your ability to be an agent of change and healing in the communities in which you live, work, worship, recreate, socialize, and serve. Guided by your integrated rule of life, you will also strengthen your abilities to love your neighbor as yourself and to express an intense love for an entire community, city, county, or country as you increase your stamina to work for solutions to social struggles. As you broaden your civic engagement, how you engage your spiritual principles and practices with those you work with and serve will mature and likely expand.

Your integrated rule of life will also help you integrate the hurts, demands, grievances, and injustices you will inevitably experience as an urban monk. Integrating these feelings into your spiritual principles and practices will continually help change troubling personal matters from sorrow to joy, and wounding societal issues from pain to healing.

The prayerful cries of the psalmist will likely become—or may have already become—similar prayers to your own because of the many steps you have taken and will continue to take.

> O God, from my youth you have taught me,
>   and I still proclaim your wondrous deeds.
> So even to old age and gray hairs,
>   O God, do not forsake me,
> until I proclaim your might
>   to all the generations to come. (Ps 71:17–18)

> We will not hide them from their children,
>   we will tell to the next generation
> the glorious deeds of the Lord and his might,
>   and the wonders that he has done. (Ps 78:4)
>
> In old age they [the righteous]
>   will still bear fruit; healthy and green. (Ps 92:14)

Encourage Others to Build Their Own

Leaving a lifelong integrated rule of life for others is a distinctive spiritual legacy, one that can help ordinary people live extraordinary lives by guiding them to nurture a deep personal and collective relationship with God in order to encounter and engage social injustices and work to end them. You can encourage others to craft their own integrated rule of life in order to be more intentional about nurturing their relationship with God and applying the fruits of that relationship to helping solve social struggles.

Others may want to learn what spiritual principles and practices you chose to integrate into your efforts as an urban monk. They may also want to know how your formative moments and experiences brought about lifelong changes in yourself and others with whom you engaged, as well as about the specific social struggles you committed to and the advancements toward solutions you helped achieve with others.

Document Your Journey

As others craft or refine their integrated rule of life, they may find it useful for you to share about your experiences in developing yours. An integrated rule of life develops over many years, so you will likely find it helpful to document your journey in a journal of some kind. You will want to include, among other things, descriptions of the social struggles you commit to, the spiritual principles and practices that sustain you in this work, obstacles on your path and what helped you overcome them, and victories you've achieved in your efforts to help others. You might also record your reflections throughout your lifetime, for example:

- When doubting that a seemingly intractable social struggle can be solved, what role did faith play in instilling confidence in you?

- What role did hope play when you faced your doubts and those of others?
- Did you forgive so that you could be forgiven?
- How have you been hurt by the social problems that you were seeking to solve?
- How might you have contributed to the social problems you were seeking to solve—for example, by inflicting hurt on others?
- How dynamic a force has humility been for you?
- How dynamic a force has grace been for you?
- How has your civic engagement brought out conflicting feelings and opinions about who deserves to benefit from a social solution?
- The grace of God is unmerited favor; it is mercy, not merit. How have you shaped your efforts to transcend the stereotypes of the deserving and the undeserving?

Share Openly and Often

As others set out to define their integrated rule of life, they may benefit from learning how you used your spiritual practices to inform and sustain your efforts and commitments to your social struggle, the communities you serve, and the people your serve with. Sharing your disciplined, convictional, and impassioned spiritual practices and how they factor into your integrated rule of life can be your legacy—and be a building block to their own legacy.

This kind of sharing can take many forms: group discussions with your congregation or as part of community meetings, formal lectures or planned speaking events, impromptu one-on-one conversations with fellow volunteers and public servants. You may find interest in hosting a rule-of-life development series in your local education centers or even online.

Through your outreach, others can learn how your convictional spiritual practices motivated and helped prepare you for community action. They may be inspired by the way your disciplined spiritual practices soothed a yearning to spend time with God and to help solve difficult social struggles. You can share how your daily dialogue with God through prayer and reading the Scriptures helped influence your approach to advancing solutions and encourage personal and societal changes. You can describe the role your relationship with God—deepened through these practices—plays in navigating the complex emotions and opinions—yours and those of others—that you encounter in your work to implement change.

By sharing your impassioned spiritual practices, you can show others how passion can be shaped into a power tool to energize civic engagement.

Adapt Your Rule of Life Annually

I encourage you to live your integrated rule of life and adapt it annually, with the ultimate goal of leaving it as your legacy. By adapt, I mean taking time out each year to closely examine and evaluate the spiritual principles and practices you have chosen and integrated into your actions to help solve social struggles. Then, consider how you can further integrate them into your civic engagement. Also take time to experience unfamiliar or new convictional or disciplined spiritual principles and practices that you might like to include in your integrated rule of life going forward. Explore new practices that are evolving out of your passion to help solve social struggles in the communities with which you engage.

The Lenten Inner Retreat Practice

I want to share a spiritual practice that I have entitled the "Lenten Inner Retreat," and I encourage you to practice it annually as an opportunity to refine your lifelong integrated rule of life. Since the earliest days of the Christian church, Lent has been associated with the forty days Christ spent in the desert before the beginning of his public ministry. By observing the forty days of Lent, you can imitate Jesus's withdrawal into the wilderness to prepare for the public ministry that is essential to helping solve social struggles.

Imitating Christ's withdrawal into an "inner desert retreat" can begin on Ash Wednesday, with a reminder that "for dust you are and to dust you will return" (Gen 3:19; Eccl 3:20) and "our days may come to seventy years, or eighty, if our strength endures" (Ps 90:10)—and hopefully longer, so we can help solve social struggles for as long as possible within our communities.

The Scriptures contain stories about others who withdrew into the desert and struggled to strengthen their relationship with God. Sometime before each Ash Wednesday, I encourage you to do as Elijah did, as described in 1 Kings 19:4–14:

> [Elijah] went a day's journey into the desert. He came to a broom tree, sat down under it and prayed that he might die. "I have had enough, Lord," he said. "Take my life; I am no better than my ancestors." Then he lay down under the tree and fell asleep.
>
> All at once an angel touched him and said, "Get up and eat." He looked around, and there by his head was a cake of bread baked over hot coals and a jar of water. He ate and drank and then lay down again. The angel of the Lord came back a second time and touched him and said, "Get up and eat, for the journey is too much for you." So he got up and ate and drank. Strengthened by that food, he traveled forty days and forty nights until he reached Horeb, the mountain of God. There he went into a cave and spent the night.
>
> And the word of the Lord came to him: "What are you doing here, Elijah?" He replied, "I have been very zealous for the Lord. . . ." The Lord said, "Go out and stand on the mountain in the presence of the Lord, for the Lord is about to pass by."
>
> Then a great and powerful wind tore the mountains apart and shattered the rocks before the Lord, but the Lord was not in the wind. After the wind there was an earthquake, but the Lord was not in the earthquake. After the earthquake came a fire, but the Lord was not in the fire. And after the fire came a gentle whisper.
>
> When Elijah heard it, he pulled his cloak over his face and went out and stood at the mouth of the cave. Then a voice said to him, "What are you doing here, Elijah?" He replied, "I have been very zealous for the Lord."

Like Elijah, may you take "a day's journey into the desert"—an inner desert—and pray. And while you are taking this journey, if you are also asked to go further until you reach "Horeb, the mountain of God," may you do so. Mount Horeb has a long history of encounters with God. It is the place where God called out to Moses from the burning bush, "I am the God of your father, the God of Abraham, the God of Isaac and the God of Jacob" and "Take off your shoes for the place where you stand is holy" (Exod 3:6, 5). It is also the place where God said to Moses, "I will stand before you upon the rock in Horeb and you shall strike the rock so that water will come out and the people shall drink" (Exod 17:6). And it is where Moses placed the Ten Commandments into the ark of the covenant (1 Kgs 8:9).

Like Elijah, may you go into the cave when you reach your own Mount Horeb and spend the night. And, like Elijah, if the Lord says to you, "What are you doing here?" may you also say, "I have been very zealous for the Lord." And if the Lord says to you, "Go out and stand on the mountain in the presence of the Lord for the Lord is about to pass by," may you listen very closely.

You may think that the presence of the Lord is near if a great and powerful wind tears the mountains apart and shatters the rocks, only to find out that the Lord is not in the wind. Or you may think that if an earthquake should follow the wind, the presence of the Lord is near, only to find out that the Lord is not. Or you may think that if a fire should follow the earthquake, the presence of the Lord is near, only to find out that the Lord is not.

However, like Elijah, you may hear a gentle whisper. And if you hear that still, small voice, may you also go out of the cave and stand at its mouth. Then may the Lord say to you a second time, as to Elijah, "What are you doing here?" May you also be able to answer the Lord a second time, "I have been very zealous for the Lord."

And while zealous for the Lord, may you begin each year a forty-day "inner desert" experience on Ash Wednesday during which you prayerfully examine your growing list of spiritual principles and practices and how you have been integrating them into your actions to solve social struggles. This will help transform your integrated rule of life into a powerful tool for solving social issues and injustices out of love for your God and your neighbors—and a blueprint for righteous living that is your legacy.

Reflection Questions

- How might you document the development of your rule of life over time so that you can easily update and adapt it, as well as pass it on to others?
- What are some ways you might share your integrated rule of life with others during your lifetime?
- Who might you share your rule of life with? Why them?

Appendix

A Lectio Divina Practice for Social Justice

THE FOLLOWING IS A lectio divina practice that includes the two steps I've added to help the urban monk connect the practice to their efforts to find solutions for seemingly intractable social struggles. It also includes more details about the practice and its roots, to provide context as you become familiar with this powerful spiritual exercise.

Reading the Word

The first step of lectio divina is appropriately called *lectio* (reading). At this point, it is important to distinguish between praying and reading. Quite simply, when we pray, we speak to God; when we read, God speaks to us. Thus, lectio is not ordinary reading. It involves *listening to* or *hearing* Scripture. More importance should be given to listening to the Word than reading it. As Benedict urges us at the beginning of his rule, "Listen, my son, and with your heart hear the principles of your Master." In his Prologue, Benedict also encourages us to let the Scriptures stir us "and attentively hear the Divine voice, calling and exhorting us." In other words, lectio is reverent listening. Our desire should be to personalize Scripture and understand the words as God speaking at that moment in time.

Within the context of lectio, reading Scripture is something different from what we normally do when we read a book. Often, we read a book for

Appendix

information or as a means of entertainment. The practice of lectio is not a monologue to God but a dialogue with God. Thus, we choose a text, read it slowly, and listen to the words closely. We read it over again and give careful attention to the literal sense of the text.

I begin lectio divina by saying, "I hear God saying to me" as a means of preparing to read the text. I often reflect on the words of wisdom given in Proverbs:

> My child, if you accept my words and treasure up my commandments within you.... (Prov 2:1)

> Listen, children, to a father's instruction, and be attentive, that you may gain insight. (Prov 4:1)

> My child, be attentive to my wisdom; incline your ear to my understanding. (Prov 5:1)

> My child, keep my words. (Prov 7:1)

I also find Proverbs 2:1–10 helpful. Try reading it slowly, again and again.

> My child, if you accept my words
>   and treasure up my commandments within you,
> making your ear attentive to wisdom
>   and inclining your heart to understanding;
> if you indeed cry out for insight,
>   and raise your voice for understanding;
> if you seek it like silver,
>   and search for it as for hidden treasures—
> then you will understand the fear of the Lord
>   and find the knowledge of God.
> For the Lord gives wisdom;
>   from his mouth come knowledge and understanding;
> He stores up sound wisdom for the upright;
>   He is a shield to those who walk blamelessly,
> guarding the paths of justice
>   and preserving the way of his faithful ones.
> Then you will understand righteousness and justice
>   and equity, every good path;
> for wisdom will come into your heart,
>   and knowledge will be pleasant to your soul.

A Lectio Divina Practice for Social Justice

Once again say, "I hear God saying to me" and begin to read your chosen text for the second time. Listen closely, for what you will soon hear is more than what the words themselves convey. Just as we convey volumes in a phrase to a loved one, so does God convey to us. You are listening to the living Word of God. Often, I am gripped by part of the text, or just a verse, and at times a phrase or a word. As I repeat these words, I hear God saying these words to me. This causes me to reflect on the meaning of the words, and it is at this point that I begin to enter into the next step: meditation.

Meditating on the Word

The second step, *meditatio* (meditation), has been described as ruminating, pondering, and pronouncing the text. Ruminating simply means chewing the cud. A cow, for example, regurgitates a mouthful of previously swallowed food and slowly chews it a second time. Thus, chewing the cud has come to mean recalling and thinking over the text.

In his Prologue, Benedict encourages us to "attentively hear the Divine voice." Remember, when you pray, you are speaking to God; when you read, God is speaking to you. So as part of meditatio, I hear the words I am reading as addressed to specifically to me. For example:

> Listen, Joseph, to (your) father's instruction,
>   and be attentive, that you may gain insight. (Prov 4:1)
>
> Joseph, be attentive to my wisdom;
>   incline your ear to my understanding. (Prov 5:1)
>
> Joseph, I have called you by name,
>   (and) you are mine. (Isa 43:1b)
>
> You are precious in my sight, Joseph,
>   and honored, and I love you. (Isa 43:4)

Thus, pondering is not meant to be a silent meditation but rather an interactive one. We take in the words through our eyes but also through our ears. When we hear God's Word, we should be willing to respond. The story of the annunciation offers such an example:

> In the sixth month the angel Gabriel was sent by God to a town in Galilee called Nazareth, to a virgin engaged to a man whose name was Joseph, of the house of David. The virgin's name was Mary. And he came to her and said, "Greetings, favored one! The

Lord is with you." But she was much perplexed by his words and pondered what sort of greeting this might be. The angel said to her, "Do not be afraid, Mary, for you have found favor with God. And now, you will conceive in your womb and bear a son, and you will name him Jesus. He will be great, and will be called the Son of the Most High, and the Lord God will give to him the throne of his ancestor David. He will reign over the house of Jacob forever, and of his kingdom there will be no end." Mary said to the angel, "How can this be, since I am a virgin?" The angel said to her, "The Holy Spirit will come upon you, and the power of the Most High will overshadow you; therefore the child to be born will be holy; he will be called Son of God. And now, your relative Elizabeth in her old age has also conceived a son; and this is the sixth month for her who was said to be barren. For nothing will be impossible with God." Then Mary said, "Here am I, the servant of the Lord, let it be with me according to your word." (Luke 1:26–38)

Praying the Word

Oratio (prayer) is our response to God. The first two steps—reading and meditating—involve God communicating to us; the words touch and awaken our hearts. In this next step, God communicates with us and we allow the words to penetrate our hearts and change our deepest selves.

Our deepest self can be changed in two ways. The first way is through love and desire, and the second way is through healing and mercy. Love and desire are two feelings that surface when we yearn to do God's will. The psalmist writes, "As a deer yearns for running streams so my soul longs for you my God" (Ps 42:1). Yearning to do God's will is fueled by our feelings of love and desire. Our feelings of love and desire are fueled by our communication with God. In the midst of such conversations, we learn what God wants to do in our lives and in the lives of others. Most notably, God wants to bring healing into the world.

Meditatio, then, brings about a two-way conversation. It brings the words of God into the innermost core of ourselves. Thus, we link our heart to God, which evokes a response from the deepest part of our inner being. Our response may include wonder, regret, surrender, and other feelings that culminate in a yearning to be in relationship with God.

Contemplating the Word

The transition to *contemplatio* (contemplation) is a result of moving further away from the experiences of thinking and talking and into the areas of feeling, sensing, loving, and intuiting. Prayer becomes a transforming power that helps us to ground ourselves in the present and to stay there. Doing so allows us to sharpen our awareness of ourselves in relationship to God, our neighbors, and ourselves.

The opposite is deadening our awareness that can come from an attempt to deliberately create a silence and stillness to rest in. Stillness and silence created by contemplation is not a quest but a result of an awareness of what God wants and our surrender to a divine embrace that does not bring knowledge but transformation.

Thus, contemplatio begins with calm acceptance of the transforming embrace of God. Transformation is needed because, if we meant what we prayed, God will penetrate our hearts with love. Such love, however, opens us up to the brokenness of all creation. It is at this point that we begin to feel that we have gone beyond the words of our texts and into a union with the divine Word.

Implementing the Word

The transition from contemplation to implementation is compassion, which is beyond sympathy. Helping to solve a social struggle involves feeling sympathetic toward others who are feeling hurt and pain caused by an injustice. We feel sorrow and concern, whereas compassion moves us to help alleviate the emotional pain of others.

Compassion not only involves alleviating the pain but preventing it from happening again. It is not a distinct emotion such as sorrow. Compassion is a response based on the loving notions of fairness, interrelationships, and justice. Thus, compassion is a variation of love.

In order to implement the Word, we must accept the transforming embrace of God, which allows God to penetrate our heart with love. To be like Christ is to embrace and yearn to help heal the hurts and pains of others. To be like Christ is to realize compassion is a variation of love but to also realize that love generates social action.

Appendix

Fulfilling the Word

Social actions fulfill the Word. Compassion as a variation of love motivates someone to take social action. Just as there are many reasons to take social action, there are many different kinds of social action we can take to help solve a social struggle. Social action can collectively help end a social struggle and prevent it from happening again.

Out of a love of neighbors or even people you may not know, you may join them to preserve an open space or to preserve something of historical or social value. You may join them to help solve local homelessness or economic disparities. You may join them to help guarantee equal social opportunities and equal protection under the law regardless of disability, gender, race, or religion.

Our social actions fulfill the Word. The more we dialogue with God and accept the transforming embrace of God while working with others to right a social wrong, the more we will treasure the Word and cry out for insight. Our social actions will remind us of God's love for humanity and that such love will guide us to continuously fulfill the Word.

Bibliography

Anonymous. *The Rule of the Master*. Translated by Charles Philippi, with an introduction by Adalbert de Vogue. Kalamazoo, MI: Cistercian, 1977.
Anthony, Susan B. *Sidewalk Contemplatives: A Spirituality for Socially Concerned Christians*. New York: Crossroad, 1987.
Augustine of Hippo. *The Rule of Saint Augustine*. Translated by Tarsicius J. Van Bavel. Kalamazoo, MI: Cistercian, 1996.
Ayida-Otobo, Alero. *Reformers Arise: Calling Out a People of Dignity to Influence and Action*. St. Albans, UK: Panoma, 2017.
Baab, Lynn. "Benedictine Spirituality: The First Vow—Stability." February 12, 2016. https://www.lynnebaab.com/blog/benedictine-spirituality-the-first-vow-s.
Barton, Ruth Haley. *Sacred Rhythms: Arranging Our Lives for Spiritual Transformation*. Downers Grove, IL: InterVarsity, 2006.
Belmonte, John. "Lectio Divina: Bridging the Gap between God's Heart and Ours." *C21 Resources*, September 1, 2008, 20–22.
Benedict of Nursia. *The Rule of St. Benedict*. Translated by Anthony C. Meisel and M. L. del Mastro. New York: Image, 1975.
Bessenecker, Scott A. *The New Friars: The Emerging Movement Serving the World's Poor*. Downers Grove, IL: InterVarsity, 2006.
Brueggemann, Walter. *The Covenanted Self: Explorations in Law and Covenant*. Minneapolis: Fortress, 1999.
Calhoun, Adele Ahlberg. *Spiritual Disciplines Handbook: Practices That Transform Us*. Downers Grove, IL: InterVarsity, 2005.
Cannon, Mae Elise. *Just Spirituality: How Faith Practices Fuel Social Action*. Downers Grove, IL: InterVarsity, 2013.
Carter, Richard. *The City Is My Monastery: A Contemporary Rule of Life*. Norwich, UK: Canterbury, 2019.
Chittister, Joan. *The Rule of Benedict: Insights for the Ages*. New York: Crossroad, 1998.
Claiborne, Shane, and Jonathan Wilson-Hartgrove. *Becoming the Answers to Our Prayers: Prayer for Ordinary Radicals*. Downers Grove, IL: InterVarsity, 2008.
Covey, Stephen. *The 7 Habits of Highly Effective People: Powerful Lessons in Personal Change*. New York: Free, 2004.
Cummings, Charles. *Monastic Practices*. Collegeville, MN: Liturgical, 2015.
Day, Dorothy, et al. *House of Hospitality*. Huntington, IN: Our Sunday Visitor, 2015.

Bibliography

De Mello, Anthony S.J. *One Minute Wisdom*. New York: Doubleday, 1985.

DeRusha, Michelle. *50 Women Every Christian Should Know: Learning from Heroines of the Faith*. Grand Rapids: Baker, 2014.

Dollen, Charles, ed. *Prayer Book of the Saints*. Huntington, IN: Our Sunday Visitor, 1984.

Driskill, Joseph D. *Protestant Spiritual Exercises: Theology, History, and Practice*. Harrisburg, PA: Morehouse, 1999.

Excellence Reporter. "Ralph Waldo Emerson: On Love, Beauty and the Purpose of Life." https://excellencereporter.com/2019/02/18/ralph-waldo-emerson-on-love-beauty-and-the-purpose-of-life/

Franck, Frederick, Janis Roze, and Richard Connolly. *What Does It Mean to Be Human? Reverence for Life Reaffirmed by Responses from around the World*. New York: St. Martin's Griffin, 2000.

Fujino, Diane C. *The Revolutionary Life of Yuri Kochiyama: Heartbeat of Struggle*. Minneapolis: University of Minnesota Press, 2005.

Garrow, David J. *Bearing the Cross: Martin Luther King, Jr., and the Southern Christian Leadership Conference*. New York: Perennial Classics, 1986.

Gungor, Ed. *The Vow: How a Forgotten Ancient Practice Can Transform Your Life*. Nashville: Thomas Nelson, 2007.

Gutiérrez, Gustavo. *We Drink from Our Own Wells: The Spiritual Journey of a People*. 1984. Reprint, Maryknoll, NY: Orbis, 2003.

Guzder, Deena. *Divine Rebels: American Christian Activists for Social Justice*. Chicago: Lawrence Hill, 2011.

Hart, Patrick. *A Monastic Vision for the 21st Century: Where Do We Go from Here?* Kalamazoo, MI: Cistercian, 2006.

Haughey, John C., ed. *The Faith That Does Justice: Examining the Christian Sources for Social Change*. New York: Paulist, 1977.

Heyer, Kristin. *Kinship across Borders: A Christian Ethic of Immigration*. Washington, DC: Georgetown University Press, 2012.

Hill, Brennan R. *8 Freedom Heroes: Changing the World with Faith*. Cincinnati, OH: St. Anthony Messenger, 2007.

Iachetta, S. Stephanie, ed. *The Daily Reader for Contemplative Living: Excerpts from the Works of Father Thomas Keating*. New York: Continuum, 2009.

"International Civil Rights Walk of Fame: Desmond Tutu: 1925–Present." National Parks Service, US Department of the Interior. https://www.nps.gov/features/malu/feat0002/wof/desmond_tutu.htm.

Isaac of Nineveh. *Mystic Treatises*. Translated by Arent Jan Wensinck. Amsterdam: Brill, 1923.

John of the Cross. *The Essential St. John of the Cross*. Translated by E. Allison Peers. Radford VA: Wilder, 2008.

King Jr., Martin Luther. *The Autobiography of Martin Luther King, Jr.* Edited by Clayborne Carson. New York: Warner Books, 1998.

———. "Desegregation and the Future." Address delivered at the Annual Luncheon of the National Committee for Rural Schools. https://kinginstitute.stanford.edu/king-papers/documents/desegregation-and-future-address-delivered-annual-luncheon-national-committee.

MacAfee, Norman, ed. *The Gospel According to RFK: Why It Matters Now*. New York: Basic, 2008.

Macchia, Stephen A. *Crafting a Rule of Life: An Invitation to the Well-Ordered Way*. Downers Grove, IL: InterVarsity, 2012.

Bibliography

Mariechild, Diane. *Open Mind: Women's Daily Inspiration for Becoming Mindful*. San Francisco: HarperSanFrancisco, 1995.

McCullough, Donald. *If Grace Is So Amazing, Why Don't We Like It?* San Francisco: Jossey-Bass, 2005.

Merton, Thomas. *Contemplative Prayer*. New York: Image, 1971.

Miller, Wendy J. *Come with Me: Daily Living with a New Monastic Rule of Life*. N.p.: Missional Wisdom Foundation, 2015.

Nouwen, Henri J. M. *Bread for the Journey: A Daybook of Wisdom and Faith*. San Francisco: HarperOne, 2006.

———. *Discernment: Reading Signs of Daily Life*. New York: HarperOne, 2013.

———. *The Wounded Healer*. New York: Image, 1979.

Paulsell, William O. *Tough Minds Tender Hearts: Six Prophets of Social Justice*. Mahwah, NJ: Paulist, 1990.

Pilarczyk, Daniel E. *Bringing Forth Justice: Basics for Just Christians*. Cincinnati, OH: St. Anthony Messenger, 1999.

Riis, Jacob A. *How the Other Half Lives*. San Bernardino, CA: ReadaClassic.com, 2010.

Ruffing, Janet K., ed. *Mysticism & Social Transformation*. Syracuse, NY: Syracuse University Press, 2001.

Rutba House. *Schools(s) for Conversion: 12 Marks of a New Monasticism*. Eugene, OR: Cascade, 2005.

Sandel, Michael J. *Justice: A Reader*. New York: Oxford University Press, 2007.

Saunders, William P. "What Is the Gift of Piety?" Catholic Straight Answers. Accessed August 1, 2024. https://catholicstraightanswers.com/gift-piety/.

Scott, Margaret. *The Eucharist and Social Justice*. Mahwah, NJ: Paulist, 2009.

Silf, Margaret. *The Gift of Prayer: Embracing the Sacred in the Everyday*. Katonah, NY: BlueBridge, 2005.

Tastard, Terry. *The Spark in the Soul: Four Mystics on Justice*. Mahwah, NJ: Paulist, 1989.

Teresa of Avila. *The Collected Works of St. Teresa of Avila, Volume Two*. Translated by Kieran Kavanaugh, O.C.D. and Otilio Rodriguez, O.C.D. Washington, DC: ICS, 1980.

———. *The Way of Perfection*. Translated and edited by E. Allison Peers. New York: Image, 1964.

Tomaine, Jane. *The Rule of Benedict: Christian Monastic Wisdom for Daily Living: Selections Annotated and Explained*. Woodstock, VT: SkyLight Paths, 2017.

"Truth Commission: South Africa." United States Institute of Peace. https://www.usip.org/publications/1995/12/truth-commission-south-africa.

"Tzedakah: Charity." Judaism 101. http://www.jewfaq.org/tzedakah.htm.

U.S. Department of Housing and Urban Development. *Fair Housing Planning Guide, Volume 1*. Washington, DC: Office of Fair Housing and Equal Opportunity, 1996.

Vest, Norvene. *Claiming Your Voice: Speaking Truth to Power*. Collegeville, MN: Liturgical, 2022.

———. *No Moment Too Small: Rhythms of Silence Prayer & Holy Reading*. Kalamazoo, MI: Cistercian, 1994.

Wallis, Jim, and Joyce Hollyday. *Cloud of Witnesses*. Washington, DC: Sojourners, 1991.

Washington, James Melvin, ed. *I Have a Dream: Writings and Speeches that Changed the World*. New York: HarperOne, 1992.

Wilson-Hartgrove, Jonathan. *New Monasticism: What It Has to Say to Today's Church*. Grand Rapids: Brazos, 2008.

www.ingramcontent.com/pod-product-compliance
Lightning Source LLC
Chambersburg PA
CBHW031618170426
43195CB00037B/1072